WALKING ON BROKEN GLASS

JANET PINKNEY

WALKING ON BROKEN GLASS

Merbune Publishing House Inc.

Dedication

Walking On Broken Glass is dedicated to the families of loved ones who are suffering from the cruel and relentless disease of addiction. It is my hope that they can use it to help put an end to generations of dysfunction and loss. Prayerfully, this book will provide the insight and wisdom needed to battle and overcome these maladies.

May Walking On Broken Glass provide a helpful recourse against these illnesses, which are currently adversely affecting our nation.

Janet Pinkney - 2026

Project Overview

*Must be something.... must be something we can do. Keep on moving, keep on moving for what's true...*Gil Scott Heron/ Brian Jackson

The objective of this book is to tie together critical elements that are essential in addressing the harsh, real threat to African Americans in the United States. These elements are crucial to our collective need to withstand the lethal combination of racism, sexism, alcoholism, drug addiction, gun violence, and soul-crushing poverty. All of which are direct manifestations of a sick society, rooted in slavery. Plainly stated, the entire nation is still in desperate need of the basics. A good sound education, and the necessity for a quality health care system that actually works. This will slow and in time, eliminate the epidemic of disease and premature death that is wreaking havoc in our communities while daily destroying lives.

The truth is out there somewhere. We owe it to ourselves to find it in our own lives and the lives of those we love. History has shown us that all is not lost. Then there is always a wild card, an element of just plain dumb luck (good or bad).

But let us suppose for a moment that we can take strong steps now that will secure our lives and the lives of our children and great-grandchildren. There is much to be gained and much to be lost in this equation. The price our ancestors paid has opened many doors, yet it is up to those of us awake and alive here and now to make what was previously impossible wholly tangible and possible.

The reality is that our children are growing up in a country where the cards have been systematically stacked against them. It's so hard not to notice, hard not to fight back like all hell breaking loose. It is our right. It is our duty, our obligation to those who fought so courageously for us to "live to see this day."

The effects of growing up black in the US have been long studied. Attention to these matters is critical to our survival as a nation.

Acknowledgements

I would like to express my sincere thanks to the following people listed below. Without them, this book would not have come into fruition.

My Lord and Savior - Jesus Christ

Celebration of Praise Life Center, Sharpsburg, GA

Dr. Evelyn Bethune - Bethune Publishing House, Inc.

The Pinkney Family

The Wright Family

The Mimi's (Gordon, Floyd)

Jean Crawford & Family

Atlanta Writers Guild

Temple University

Habitat for Humanity

American Kidney Foundation

Piedmont Hospital, Fayetteville, GA

Dr. Georgia Theriot

Dr. Nicole Sroka

Dr. Nicole Quinn

Dr. Thelma Wiley Lucas

Charles E. Williams

CONTENTS

PROLOGUE

It seems like you know just about everything. Once you hit your 50s and 60s, nothing can take you by surprise. Yet that's not entirely true. I was caught off guard, completely unprepared for what came in July 2023.

I was asleep when the phone rang. I still kept a landline for backup, just in case my lazy cell phone didn't work. I rolled over in my big, comfortable king-size bed and picked it up on the second ring, totally unprepared for what I was about to hear.

Screaming. Yelling in the background. I slid off the bed onto the floor, clinging to the phone, straining to hear what the hell was going on.

All I could make out was, "Sean's dead... Sean's dead..."

Sean who? I had just spoken with my son the day before, and he was fine. What Sean? Certainly not my Sean, my only son. Say again?

A voice came over the phone that I didn't recognize, though I could hear my daughter Saida, screaming his name in the background. It was his girlfriend, Karen, who had come to visit Sean that night and found him in bed, dead.

Loud heavy footsteps echoed through the line. I asked Karen if the police were there and to put them on the phone.

"I'm sorry, Ma'am, but your son is dead. We don't know for how long. The paramedics are taking him directly to the morgue in Cobb County. He is dead," the officer repeated.

Karen came back on the line while Sean's sister continued to scream his name in the background. I asked to speak to Saida, who was inconsolable. I spoke softly, trying to calm her down long enough to figure out what was happening. I told her I was on my way. She lived over 50 miles away, so I ran around my house throwing clothes into an overnight bag, half believing what I had just heard.

I called my partner and dear friend of 30 years, Charles Willams, and asked him to call me on my cell. Driving crazy at dawn, I was already out of the door. I told him the grim news and asked him to meet me at the MARTA rail line in College Park for the long drive to my daughter's house. I don't remember the drive there.

I do remember that Charles showed up for me once again, for what seemed like the thousandth time, to bear witness to yet another heartbreak, another tragedy, another death, endured by a family that had already seen too much heartache and grief. The crying game.

Sean was only 52 when he died suddenly of a massive stroke.

He had suffered two previous strokes; the second one, he and his sister tried to keep from me. Included with the terrible grief and loss was the hard-edged feeling that his death could have been prevented, coupled with unspeakable anger.

I no longer recognized the woman I saw in the mirror. Broken and beaten after all I had endured to bring him into this world. All that I had endured, all of my efforts to raise him healthy, safe, and secure in an unwelcome, often violent society, it seemed like such a waste.

And it was.....

SEAN

MY SOUL LOOKS BACK

M y Soul Looks Back

Sometimes my soul looks back and wonders how I got over

Mahalia Jackson

Sean had called me just two days earlier, complaining about the heat, talking about his plans to visit his daughter in New York. He'd sounded tired but not sick, frustrated but surely not dying, just a normal everyday conversation.

But Sean had been dying for years, slowly and stubbornly, from the same fragile health that had marked him from birth. I ran through the house, cutting on all the lights, as if somehow the brightness could awaken me from this nightmare, forcing its way into my life. First hot, then cold, then nothing. I didn't cry, didn't scream. Maybe I was too shocked, too afraid to believe what I'd just heard was true.

I opened the back door and peered out into the dark July sky, the same sky I'd left behind in my dreams just minutes before. At least the stars were still there. The familiar sounds of crickets and frogs reminded me that the world was still turning, although I was no longer in it.

My conscience stood silently aside and watched from a distance as my carefully constructed world came to a stone-cold halt. My life as I had known it vanished suddenly, just like that, snap, all over, all gone.

I felt like a two-bit actor in an old black-and-white "B" movie. Something was terribly wrong, something was strangely, absolutely, wrong.

The feeling was akin to watching pigs fly. Of course, this cannot be happening; this was not real. My mind was reeling as I tried desperately to make sense of what I'd just heard. How can this be real?

Surely God would not be so cruel as to take my only son from me forever. But as I stood there in my old T-shirt, shivering despite the summer heat, I knew this was real. And I knew that Sean's death was the final chapter in a story that had begun fifty-two years earlier, when a teenage girl fought to bring a fragile baby into the world and spent the rest of her life trying to keep him alive.

The Fight That Started at Birth

Sean's health had been precarious from the moment he drew his first breath. Born underweight and struggling, he came into the world fighting a pattern that would define both our lives for the next five decades.

As a baby, he was plagued with chronic asthma that could turn life-threatening without warning. When other children got immunized, they might feel a little under the weather. When Sean got his shots, he'd contract whatever disease he was being protected against — mumps, measles, chicken pox, you name it. If a kid got a cold at daycare, Sean caught it and ended up in the emergency room.

Einstein Medical Center became our second home. Three miles from our house in Philadelphia, it was our sanctuary when Sean's breathing turned labored, when his fever spiked, when the world became a dangerous place for a little boy whose lungs couldn't do their job properly.

We made that journey at least two or three times a month, sometimes more. When I had money, we took a cab. Most of the time, we walked — me half-carrying a sick child through the streets of Philadelphia, racing against his next asthma attack.

Eventually, the ER staff knew us by name. We no longer had to wait in line or fumble for insurance cards. Sean would be whisked back to the nurses' station, where he was greeted with warmth and professional concern. For a terrified young mother with a chronically ill child, that hospital became an oasis of help and compassion.

Sean was a remarkably good patient. He never complained about the needles or the ice baths they used to bring down his fevers. He endured treatments that would make adults cringe, but he accepted them with a stoicism that broke my heart and filled me with pride.

Because I was still an undergraduate at Temple University, I usually brought my textbooks and notes to the hospital. I'd study throughout the night while monitors tracked my son's breathing, often with an exam or paper due the next day. It often took until dawn for his lungs to clear enough for us to go home.

One summer, he remained hospitalized for several weeks — almost the entire vacation. I visited every day, bringing him home-cooked meals and trying to make a sterile hospital room feel like the safe haven he needed. Fortunately, it happened during my break from classes, so I could be there constantly without falling behind academically.

When Sean was about 7 or eight years old, he was well enough to be home but too sick for daycare, I had to leave him alone, secured with a long phone cord by his side. This was the 1970s — no cordless phones, no cell phones, no microwave to heat up quick meals. I'd call between classes, listening carefully to the sound of his breathing, then rush home on the subway, often stopping to buy special treats to brighten his day.

His sister Saida was just a toddler then, and she'd stay with the babysitter while I tended to Sean's medical needs. I always felt a rush of relief and pure joy just seeing him safe and sound when I finally made it home. Those moments of gratitude became the foundation of everything I would later understand about love, sacrifice, and the fierce protectiveness that defines motherhood.

The Dream of Normal

Sean was the main reason I married his father, Jeff. I wanted desperately to give my children what I'd had growing up: a normal life with two parents, a stable home, the security of family. I adored my son and genuinely loved his father, at least in the beginning. Sean was my guiding light, my motivation for every difficult decision I made.

I fought like hell to keep him healthy throughout his childhood and beyond. Even as an adult, Sean would speak fondly of growing up in our house on Wagner Avenue. In fact, when his daughter, born years later, was given the middle name "Wagner" Alexis Wagner after the street where he'd experienced whatever childhood normalcy his health allowed.

When Sean married his childhood sweetheart, Marlayna, the two moved to New York. I supported the decision completely. He was a grown man who needed to take responsibility for his own life and health. Marlayna was a wonderful addition to our family. I'd known her since she was fourteen and had taken her under my wing the way other women had done for me years before. She understood Sean's medical needs and loved him despite his challenges.

But Sean was careless with the life I'd fought so hard to protect. Poor diet, fast food, binge drinking, smoking, all the habits that were particularly dangerous for someone with his medical history. He resisted my advice and warnings. Even his doctors couldn't convince him to take his health seriously.

The Strokes That Stole My Son

The first stroke hit when Sean was forty-three. We were having our usual Sunday morning phone call when he suddenly felt ill. I told him to hang up immediately and dial 911. Hours later, he called from Yale Medical Center in Connecticut to tell me he'd had a major stroke affecting his entire right side. He had lost the ability to speak and the simple act of walking was difficult.

I was on a plane within days. His X-wife Marlayna, and her sister Shannon met me at the hospital, while I navigated the insurance maze. Although he had a job, he had no health insurance. I brought along my laptop and filed an emergency application for disability insurance. In the meantime, it took several weeks in the hospital before Sean could begin the long process of recovering his speech and mobility. His eyesight had also been adversely affected.

But even a stroke couldn't convince him to change his lifestyle, which could have saved his life.

The second stroke came a few years later, after Sean had moved back to Georgia to live with his sister. This time, he and Saida decided not to tell me, perhaps to spare me worry, perhaps because they knew I'd try to intervene again. I only learned about it after he'd been discharged. The third stroke, in July 2023, took his life.

THE POISON OF ABSENT FATHERS

Part of Sean's self-destructive behavior, I knew, came from the poison his father Jeff had been feeding him for decades. Jeff never missed an opportunity to disrespect me or slander me to our son, gossiping like a schoolgirl and telling Sean stories that were either partially true or outright lies.

While I had moved on with my life in Atlanta, Jeff was still living with his mother in middle age, nursing grievances and teaching Sean that real men don't listen to women, even women who are trying to save their lives.

I understood Jeff's damage. He'd lost his father at an early age and had never received the therapy that might have helped him process that trauma. Raised by a hardworking mother who had to support five boys alone, Jeff never learned what healthy masculinity looked like. He didn't know how to be a man, much less a father.

But understanding Jeff's brokenness didn't excuse the damage he did to our son. When parents use their children as weapons against each other, they poison young minds with bitterness and resentment; the children pay the price sometimes with their very lives.

No child should hear his mother called names by his own father. No child should be taught that asking for help is weakness, that taking care of your health is unmanly, that the women who love you are enemies rather than allies.

A Legacy of Love and Loss

As I stood in my kitchen that July morning, surrounded by the silence that follows devastating news, I thought about the broader context of Sean's death. He wasn't just my son; he was one of countless Black men who die too young from preventable causes, victims of a culture that teaches boys to ignore pain, avoid doctors, and equate vulnerability with weakness.

Sean's death was part of a larger tragedy affecting African American families across the country, the epidemic of early death that leaves mothers childless, children fatherless, and communities devastated. It's the price we pay for growing up in a country where being Black and male means carrying invisible wounds that never heal properly.

This book is written in honor of Sean and all the sons, brothers, fathers, mothers, sisters, and loved ones we've lost too soon. It's written for the families who have endured these tragedies and somehow found the strength to carry on. It's written because we all need to comprehend the truth about the human costs it takes to survive in a world that has historically disenfranchised and forced Black families apart.

But most of all, it's written because Sean's life, complicated, frustrating, and ultimately too short, mattered. The little boy who endured countless medical procedures without complaint, who fought for every breath, who taught me what unconditional love really means, deserved a better ending than the one he got.

And maybe, by telling his story honestly, I can help other sons make different choices, other mothers fight different battles, other families break the cycles that claimed too many people I've loved.

HOT SUMMERTIME

---

*T*he Telephone Wars

Hot Summertime and the living is easy... your daddy's rich and your mama's good looking... hush little baby don't you cry. - From Porgy and Bess

The foundation of who I became was laid in the hands of a woman who refused to let the world diminish her, no matter what it took away. My grandmother, Mamie Fuller Pinkney, Mom-Mom to everyone who mattered, was the family matriarch whose word was law and whose love shaped everything I understood about strength, strategy, and survival.

My earliest lessons in power dynamics came from an old-fashioned black dial phone on the second-floor landing of our house on Marion Avenue. Whenever I got into trouble, which was often, since I was a three-year-old terror with an advanced understanding of manipulation, I would run like hell to that phone and furiously dial Mom-Mom's number: CE28241.

I'd jump up and down impatiently, watching the dial rotate slowly around each number, hoping to reach her before my mother could catch me and deliver the spanking I'd earned. If I succeeded in getting Mom-Mom on the line and pleading my case fast enough, she would talk my mother out of punishing me. If I failed, I got my butt whipped.

I quickly realized that my mother had no real authority over me compared to Mom-Mom's power. As the family matriarch, Mom-Mom's word was final. She loved me fiercely, my only granddaughter, her partner in crime, the child people said looked just like her.

That resemblance was fine with me; Mom-Mom was a beautiful woman with fair skin and long dark hair. She carried the kind of presence that commanded respect wherever she went.

My strategy worked perfectly until the day my plan backfired. Instead of our usual kitchen routine, my mother making fresh bread while I played at her feet, rolling dough and smelling the warm yeast rolls baking my mother snatched me up to eye level, my legs dangling, and delivered a message I'd never forget: "If you tell your daddy on me again, I'm gonna whip your ass, and I mean good." Then she proceeded to do exactly that.

That spanking did not shut down my telephone scam permanently, but it also taught me something crucial about power: even the strongest people have limits, and pushing someone too far can backfire dramatically.

The Woman Who Shaped My World

Mom-Mom's real name was Mamie Fuller Pinkney, and she carried herself like royalty despite the hardships that had marked her life. She was a professional seamstress who worked for herself, creating beautiful clothes for weddings, special events, and everyone appreciated her exceptional skill. Her work never looked homemade; every stitch was perfect, every detail exactly right.

But Mom-Mom's true talent was teaching me how to navigate the world as a Black girl who refused to be invisible. She dressed me in outfits that announced my presence and took me everywhere she went, on shopping trips on the 23 trolley to downtown Philadelphia's major department stores like Gimbels, Wanamaker's, and Woolworth's.

I loved those expeditions, especially riding the wooden escalators and exploring the vast fabric departments with their bewildering arrays of bolted cloth. Mom-Mom would let me choose patterns from Vogue, Simplicity, and Butterick, then select fabrics that would make me look like the little princess she believed I was.

Back home, her small apartment would fill with the smells of homemade cakes and pies while she created custom outfits that made other little girls stare.

During summers, she made what she called my "jumping outfits" cute sets that tied with strings at the shoulders, complete with matching silk ribbons. Even my play clothes were tailored to perfection. While my brothers came to visit often, I was essentially raised by Mom-Mom while my mother worked for "the white folks," whoever the hell they were.

When my mother would ask for a full accounting of my behavior, Mom-Mom would cover for me every time. "She was no trouble, Nervie," she'd say, using her nickname for my mother, whose real name was Minerva.

This protection taught me the value of people who love you unconditionally, and how that love shielded you from consequences you've earned, a lesson that would serve me well in different seasons of my life.

The Easter Dress Rebellion

The incident that perfectly captured Mom-Mom's influence on my developing personality happened at Easter when I was six years old. As usual, Mom-Mom decided to make my Easter dress, and as usual, I was allowed to choose the style, color, and accessories.

That year, my favorite color was red. Mom-Mom created a stunning, bright red organdy dress with white ruffles that fit me perfectly.

We completed the ensemble with a red hat, red shoes, white lacy ankle socks, and a cute little red purse. I felt like a movie star.

The problem emerged when we met my parents at church. My mother stopped us at the church door, her mouth falling open in shock and dismay. There I was, dressed head-to-toe in bright red on Easter Sunday, the day Christians celebrate Jesus Christ's resurrection.

In my mother's understanding, wearing red on Easter was disrespectful to the crucifixion, since red represented the blood Jesus shed on the cross. I was completely unaware of this symbolism and stood proudly in my beautiful outfit while Mom-Mom gently held my hand, and my mother shot daggers at us from across the sanctuary.

The congregation stared, whispered, and probably judged, but Mom-Mom never wavered. She squeezed my hand reassuringly and let me know that sometimes being different, being bold, being exactly who you are, is more important than following rules that don't make sense to you.

That Easter dress taught me about confidence, about the power of presentation, and about having people in your corner who will support your right to take up space in the world, even when others disapprove.

Lessons in Rebellion and Beauty

Mom-Mom's influence extended beyond clothes into more permanent expressions of my developing independence. When I was about nine, during one of my extended stays at her house, we conspired to pierce my ears without my mother's permission.

My mother, raised in the South, believed pierced ears made a woman look "loose" the same way many people today view certain types of body modification. But Mom-Mom had pierced ears and a stunning collection of gold and silver earrings that I played with constantly. Why shouldn't I have the same options?

We both knew my mother would disapprove, but we did it anyway. When she came to pick me up that weekend, I had two white strings hanging from my little ears, along with peroxide and Vaseline to prevent infection. Mom-Mom had given me my first pair of solid gold earrings, which I promptly lost down the bathroom drain.

My father took apart the entire sink, trying to find that earring while my mother fumed. But after my considerable crying and screaming, the earrings were replaced with another solid gold pair.

The message was clear: when you know what you want, and you have powerful allies, you can usually find a way to get it.

THE SHADOW OF LOSS

The Shadow of Loss

What I didn't understand as a child was how so much loss had shaped Mom-Mom's fierce protection. She had lost an infant daughter named Marie to pneumonia many years before I was born. I could hear the pain in her voice, the few times she mentioned it, and I realized later that perhaps she saw me as her second chance to love and protect a little girl.

Mom-Mom also carried the weight of her husband's violent death. My grandfather August had been ambushed and killed in Savannah by his mistress's brothers when my father was just twelve years old. According to Mom-Mom, the woman was so devastated by his death that she jumped to her own death, killing the baby she was carrying.

Mom-Mom told me she attended that woman's funeral, where the dead infant lay nestled in her mother's arms in the casket.

It was one of the last stories she shared before she died, and I understood then that much of her life had been spent trying to overcome that trauma, to create love and stability from the ashes of violence and betrayal.

The Diabetes That Defined Us

As Mom-Mom aged, diabetes began to claim parts of her body. She injected herself with insulin daily, refusing to let the disease defeat her spirit even as it took her right leg. The hospital gave her a prosthesis and wheelchair, both of which she despised. Instead, she insisted on using a crutch and continued living independently until her death.

Her courage in the face of progressive disability was remarkable. She never complained about the tough hand life had dealt her, never gave in to self-pity or despair. When she needed help with errands or household chores, she'd call me or my younger brother Eric. I gladly provided whatever assistance I could.

What I didn't understand then was that diabetes would become a family curse, claiming almost all of Mom-Mom's grandchildren, including me. Black Americans are twice as likely to develop diabetes as the general population, and in our family, the disease would later take my brother Robert through a series of agonizing amputations.

But watching Mom-Mom face her illness with dignity taught me lessons about grace under pressure that would serve me well when I faced my own health challenges decades later.

The Legacy of Strength

Mom-Mom died when I was in my twenties, but her influence on my character was permanent. She taught me that being loved unconditionally gives you the foundation to take risks, to be bold, to refuse to make yourself smaller for other people's comfort.

She showed me that style and presentation matter not because appearance is everything, but because how you present yourself to the world affects how the world treats you. She demonstrated that strategic thinking and loving protection aren't mutually exclusive; you can shield someone from consequences while still teaching them how to navigate complex social dynamics.

Most importantly, Mom-Mom proved that women could be formidable forces who commanded respect through competence, dignity, and the kind of love that refuses to accept limitations others try to impose.

The little girl who wore a red dress to Easter service, who got her ears pierced despite her mother's objections, who learned to work the phone system to avoid punishment, grew into a woman who understood that sometimes you have to break rules to create the life you deserve.

Mom-Mom's lessons about power, presentation, and protection would guide me through teenage pregnancy, failed marriages, educational challenges, and eventually into the kind of strategic thinking that allowed me to build something lasting for my own children.

Her legacy wasn't just the love she gave me, but the model she provided for how to be a woman who refuses to be defeated, no matter what life takes away from you. I still wear pierced earrings and think of her often.

MY BROTHERS

My Brothers

As the night turns cold and the stars look down, and you find yourself on the cold, cold ground. You wait for morning in a stranger's coat; no one would you see. You ask yourself who'd watch for me, your only friend, who could it be? I hate to say it. I hate to say it, but it's probably me - Sting

The Brotherhood That Built Me

Growing up as the only girl among six brothers taught me everything I needed to know about love, protection, loyalty, and the complex dynamics of relationships. Each of my brothers showed me different aspects of what it meant to be cherished, challenged, and defended. Their love shaped my personality and my understanding of how I deserved to be treated by the world.

Being surrounded by boys could have made me tough in many ways; they taught me to compete as an option rather than collaborate, and how to fight in order to achieve the results I want. My brothers created a cocoon of protection and love that allowed me to develop confidence without hardness, strength without defensiveness.

Eric: The Baby Brother Who Wasn't

Eric was five years younger than I, but somehow, I remained "baby sister" even after he was born. This wasn't about age; it was about position, about the special place I held in our family hierarchy as the only girl.

Eric quickly learned the ropes from his older brothers about how to be a lovable pain in the ass. He'd tease me about being "baby sister" while pulling pranks that would have gotten him killed if he'd tried them on anyone else. But Eric also shared my passion for music, and we'd spend hours listening to R&B while I interpreted the emotional meaning behind the songs. Later, his favorite Teena Marie, and he'd play her music while I explained what she really meant when she sang about love and heartbreak.

One memorable day, all my brothers decided it would be hilarious to pop the heads off my dolls and switch them around. They thought this prank was comedy gold until my father came home and saw what they'd done. He immediately put a lock on my bedroom door and forbade any of them from entering my private space.

For the moment, my belongings were safe. Then my brothers soon learned to pick the lock, and the games began again. But the message was clear: I was special, my space was sacred, and anyone who violated that would face consequences.

June: My Irish Twin and Partner in Crime

June and I were born almost exactly two years apart, but we were so close in size and temperament that people often referred to us as one entity: "JanetandJune." We were both Sagittariuses, both stubborn, both passionate about everything we did. We loved each other fiercely and fought constantly, sometimes tumbling downstairs together and getting up to continue our argument.

As we got older, June and I became travel companions, dressing alike and double-dating around town. For my senior prom, we even went as a foursome; June's date was my classmate, nick-named Fuzzy, because of her halo of curly dark hair. After prom, the four of us drove to New York for the weekend, pretending we were sophisticated adults instead of teenagers playing dress-up.

June taught me about true partnership, about having someone who would stand with you even when you were wrong, who would defend you against the world even when you probably de-served whatever trouble you'd gotten into.

Brook: My Hero and Protector

Booker T, we called him Brook, was my absolute favorite, though I tried not to show it too obviously. Named after Booker T. Wash-ington, he carried himself with a dignity that I thought was so-phisticated, though I initially considered his name old-fashioned, given my newly enlightened views on civil rights.

Brook and I looked remarkably alike, and we often declared our-selves the "pick of the litter", the best-looking, most charming siblings in the family. We spent countless hours together dream-ing about our future lives, about the "boss cribs" we'd live in without meddling parents, about all the adventures we'd have as adults.

He was the brother who taught me to tie my shoes when I was three, who let me tag along on his paper route, who allowed me to play with my paper dolls in his bedroom when the other brothers had banished me from their space. Brook was sensitive, loving, and fiercely protective, especially when it came to me.

When my husband, Jeff, became abusive and violent in my life years later, Brook was the brother who kicked his ass more than once. He always had my back, always defended me against any threats, real or imagined. In his eyes, I could do no wrong, and his unconditional love gave me a foundation of security that would sustain me through decades of challenge and change.

Brook later married his lovely wife, Mimi, and had a daughter named Chanda. When Chanda had her own daughter, she named her Brooke in honor of the grandfather who'd shown our extended family what protective love looked like.

Mimi's family truly loved Brook and their role in his life, and mine was special, maybe divine. We remain close until this very day. Brook also claimed my son Sean as his own, crowning him "Prince" of the family and maintaining a relationship that gave Sean some of the most positive male role models in his life.

Robert: The Physical Brother

Robert was positioned as the oldest, which made him responsible for all of us whenever our parents were away. He was also the first to have a serious girlfriend, Sheila Ransome, his childhood sweetheart, whom he married at eighteen.

Robert's physicality was playful and affectionate. Robert was good with his hands and had built an elaborate Morse code system from his third-floor bedroom down to the first-floor foyer. He was physical in his interactions, especially with me.

As soon as he saw me, the chase would begin, he'd pursue me around the house until he caught me, then throw me down and tickle me until I screamed "uncle." He continued this practice even after we became adults.

The children would laugh with anticipation as soon as they saw him. They knew that when Uncle Robert showed up, the race was on. It didn't matter where we were, public or private, I would get tackled and tickled.

Robert had swagger like Barry White, lots of charisma, and energy that made him popular with everyone, especially women. He was married several times throughout his life, always looking for someone who could match his intensity and zest for life.

The Vietnam War

I worried constantly about my older brother James and my uncle Greg, who had been drafted into the Vietnam War. I'd watch Walter Cronkite read the nightly casualty reports and pray that my brother's name wouldn't be among them.

We wrote to each other regularly, and the mail took about two weeks each way. I followed the anti-war protests with the intensity of someone who had personal stakes in the conflict, which, of course, I did.

James was generous and kind, often buying gifts for me and my girlfriends, Whitman chocolates, transistor radios, and movie tickets. One day after he was discharged from the Army, I came home from school to find he'd bought me a white bunny rabbit I named Fluffy. Fluffy lived in a converted cabinet in our backyard for several years, and I treasured the rabbit and the thoughtfulness behind the gift.

Everyone loved James, young and old, family and friends. My mother relied on him heavily to get things done and to provide stability for the younger children.

Clarence: The Gentle Giant

Clarence was much older than me and had a stutter that made him speak carefully and thoughtfully. He called me "Miss Janet" with a formality that made me feel respected and important. Clarence would take me to playgrounds and carnivals, patient with my endless energy and curiosity.

He married young and had a lovely family, his wife Edith and three beautiful children, Leslie, Clarence, and Christine. Clarence was a simple man who didn't require much to be happy. He was quick to laugh and slow to anger; I never saw him lose his temper with anyone.

Despite being significantly older, Clarence never hesitated to help when any of us needed support. He understood that family meant showing up, even when it was inconvenient, even when the problems weren't his to solve.

WORTH IT

The Architecture of Love

Living with six brothers taught me lessons I couldn't have learned any other way. They were responsible for me wherever we went—church, school, the park, anywhere we ventured as a family. If I came home with so much as a scratch, there was hell to pay. They took this responsibility seriously, understanding that my safety reflected on their character as men and brothers.

As they became teenagers and started dating, they faced a significant problem: me. They had to take their baby sister along on dates, which they hated but accepted as part of their family obligations. They'd bribe me with concession stand food to sit quietly in the back row while they kissed their girlfriends, and I happily accepted these terms. I saw all the latest movies and ate all the candy and hot dogs I wanted; it was definitely a win-win situation.

The house itself reflected my special status. My brothers shared a large two-bedroom suite with single beds for each of them, while I had my own room, complete with a closet full of clothes, nice furniture, and frilly curtains that announced this space belonged to someone precious. I was never a tomboy, never had to compete for resources or space, never doubted that I was treasured.

The Foundation for Everything

Each brother taught me different aspects of love and protection. From Eric, I learned about playful affection and shared interests. From June, I understood partnership and loyalty. Brook showed me unconditional acceptance and fierce protection. Robert demonstrated that physical strength could be gentle and fun. James provided cultural education and generosity. Clarence modeled dignity and consistent kindness.

Together, they created an environment where I felt completely secure in my identity as someone worthy of protection, care, and respect. They showed me what it looked like when men prioritized my well-being, when my happiness mattered more than their convenience, when love was expressed through action rather than just words.

This foundation of security would serve me well in different seasons of my life. It gave me the confidence to take risks, to expect respect, to refuse to accept less than I deserved. But it also made me vulnerable to men who didn't understand that loving someone meant protecting them, supporting them, and showing up consistently even when life got difficult.

The boys who grew up determined to keep their baby sister safe created a woman who knew her worth, even when circumstances temporarily made her forget it. Their love was the template against which I would measure every relationship that followed, the standard that eventually helped me recognize real love when it finally appeared in my life.

My brothers gave me the most precious gift possible: the unshakable knowledge that I was worthy of love, protection, and loyalty. That knowledge would carry me through decades of challenge and change, reminding me during my darkest moments that I came from people who valued me simply for existing, who would move heaven and earth to keep me safe.

It was the kind of love that creates warriors, women who know they're worth fighting for since birth.

A CHANGE IS GONNA COME

*G*rowing Up In Philadelphia

It's been a long, long time coming, but I know a change is gonna come – Sam Cooke

In the summer of 1964, Philly had a riot. It started when the police assaulted a young man on Columbia Ave (now Cecil B. Moore). The riot lasted for 3 days. The angry crowd looted and destroyed mostly white-owned businesses. Hundreds of people were injured or arrested, and two people died. According to the local newspaper, The Philadelphia Daily News, 726 buildings had been hit hard.

The vast majority of the businesses were owned by Jewish merchants, who sold groceries, appliances, and furniture. Ultimately, all of the businesses were adversely affected. Mommy kept us locked up inside our house. I wasn't scared; I was curious. What was the riot about anyway? Why were people so angry?

After the riot, we were forbidden to go down to Columbia Ave, a once-thriving business community. Although we lived several blocks away, we could hear the chaos, loud sounds of broken glass, gunfire, and the rancid smell of smoke everywhere.

When we finally walked down Columbia Ave, the streets were deserted and destroyed. Broken windows, glass everywhere, boarded-up buildings, and lots of trash strewn about.

Before the riot, the area was prosperous, with all types of businesses, movie theaters, beauty parlors, barber shops, and record stores. The businesses were all effectively destroyed. Thus, ending an era of prosperity and the beginning of blight and poverty in our neighborhood. The area tried in vain to make a comeback, but it never fully recovered.

The next summer, my mother took us all to a freedom march led by Dr. Martin Luther King, Jr. in August 1965. I was 10 years old. The march was centered around Girard College, a private school for white orphan boys only. It was situated smack dab in the middle of a black neighborhood in North Philly.

I watched intensely as Dr. King spoke, the crowd roaring its approval. Thousands of black people were there, as well as local news outlets.

I had never been in a crowd that large in my young life. Soon, I began reading everything I could get my hands on. I read letters from San Quentin Jail. I soon understood why my parents could not or would not explain racism and segregation to me.

A history of treachery, murder, and deceit is a tough pill to swallow, much less explain to a curious child. I would swipe copies of Muhammad Speaks from anywhere I could get a copy, mostly from well-dressed 'brothers' who wore bow ties and hawked the newspaper on ghetto streets.

Then in comes Muhammad Ali. My dad called him a 'big mouth', but I loved him for it. One ordinary summer afternoon, he came to my neighborhood, a crowd of people gathering on the street to touch him and converse with him. It was just after his win with Sonny Liston. It was our win as well. We were so proud of him. I ran home screaming.

Muhammad Ali is around the corner. Although all my siblings were at home, only one of my brothers came. Booker T., we used to share this memory and laugh about this pretty often. I touched his shoulder, and this giant of a man turned to smile down on me. Suddenly, being black was the thing to be! I came alive in that moment.

I listened keenly for clues and other information that would lead me to a better understanding of how this terrible tragedy had befallen so many good, innocent black people (much less me personally). I no longer trusted God. How could he let this lie go on for so long, 400 years, and black folks still at the bottom?

I became an eleven-year-old hot-head revolutionary. I read the autobiography of Malcolm X several times, as soon as I could get my hands on my own copy.

That year, my parents rented a large 3-story house at the corner of 24th & Thompson St. My bedroom was on the 2nd floor, next to the bathroom. Of course, there was always my trusted friend, the black telephone, which still stood like a sentry on the 2nd floor landing.

I loved my room and soon filled it with pictures of my favorite groups. I had a best friend, Helen Clark, who had a brother named

Topaz. We spent many hours in my room playing with my dolls and listening to WDAS and WIBG on my transistor radio.

I was now in John Wanamaker Junior High School and had fallen in love with music. The Motown sound became my bible, my church. Let's not forget Atlantic, out of New York (which had Aretha Franklin), and Stax Records out of Tennessee, which produced Otis Redding, Issac Hayes, and Booker T. and The MG's. This music made a profound impression on me (as it did most people). Those songs still resonate with me today.

What is all this love stuff all about anyway, and why did everybody want it? These talented artists were somehow able to communicate not only the words and melody, but what it actually feels like to be in their shoes. True art.

I graduated from the 6th grade at John F. Reynolds in the spring of 1967; my parents were so proud. I received an award for outstanding academic achievement, and I was hooked on academics. But something was changing at home.

My father's drinking was getting worse. More nights, he came home late, or didn't come home at all. The arguments between my parents grew louder and more frequent. Mommy would try to keep us upstairs, away from it, but we heard everything in that house.

I guess my childhood ended right there in that house. Somehow, I discovered that I was a 'colored girl', a 'negro', different from the population at large, a problem to be solved, unwanted, unknown, someone to be dismissed, unheard. Philly was a hotbed of civil unrest, much like the rest of the country at that time.

That fall, everything fell apart. My parents had yet another terrible fight due to my dad's drinking, but this one was different.

This time, he got violently drunk, and my mother had him arrested. I witnessed the whole thing, me, my brothers, and the entire neighborhood. The fight was very loud and very public. The police, the screaming, the blood. My father (who always carried a switchblade knife) had cut my mother on her right arm very badly. I was sad, scared, and embarrassed.

The Uptown

Shortly thereafter, we moved into the same apartment building that my grandmother lived in, the 'projects'. The projects didn't have the stigma that they do now. It was actually viewed as a desirable place to live, with clean lawns, scheduled maintenance, and no crime. It was not a slum, but rather a welcome refuge for families who needed decent housing with no place else to go.

My brothers and I had started going to the fabulous Uptown Theater on Broad St, a few blocks away from our 3-bedroom apt on Diamond St in the projects. The DJs at WDAS and WHAT were local heroes: Butterball, Jerry Blavat (the Geter with the heater), Georgie Woods (the man with the goods). They brought local talent that became cultural icons: The Delphonics, The Dells, Jerry Butler, the Five Stair Steps, Patti LaBelle and the Blue Bells, Unifics, The O'Jays, Mad Lads, Billy Stewart, Contours, Brenda and the Tabulations, and many others.

My heart would fill with the emotion of their songs, the joy and heartbreak of being in and out of love. All these acts got their start at the Uptown, a real showcase for up-and-coming talent. These amazing, talented folks did not stop performing until the entire audience was on their feet. Patty La Belle and the O'Jays were famous for that.

I remember seeing Miss Patti backstage and her fans teasing her about her tendency to kick off her high heels and roll around singing on the stage floor. She couldn't have been much older than we were. We used to tell her that she would never be accepted in polite society, making moves like that. Today, she is famous worldwide for her passion and willingness to share her heart with millions of people, short on hope.

Yes, even the Jackson 5 came to the Uptown. I was an autograph hound along with my best friend, Sarah Jane. We would stand at the stage door and hit up the performers for autographs. I almost knocked Michael Jackson down to get a glimpse of his brother Jermaine.

I witnessed amazing talent week after week, and was so very impressed. Live bands, singing, and dancing, OMG. Like the Apollo, in NYC, if you can make it there, you can make it anywhere. How we loved them. Followed their every word, duplicated their dance steps, and their emotional gestures.

At the time, I had no idea that this was history in the making. When those groups came to TV on the Ed Sullivan show, we were excited, surprised, and shocked. Black people were rarely seen on television. For the first time in American history, black life was being celebrated worldwide, and we didn't care who dug it.

Every weekend after our chores, we were metered out a small allowance, maybe two or three dollars to spend how we liked. My brothers took odd jobs, paper routes, farm labor in NJ, whatever they could get. Looking back, I don't know how my mother did it, with her meager wages as a domestic, but she did it.

We never had a hungry day. A true act of raw courage, rarely seen today. I always felt secure with my grandmother downstairs at apartment A-1.

My father was still a big part of my life; we saw him on some weekends. He was living with a woman named Curlie, who let him drink to his heart's content. My mother never said a bad word about my father, even though he was clearly at fault for their breakup. They never divorced. In the meantime, she even bought Father's Day cards, having each of us sign the cards and send them to my father.

Despite his shortcomings, my mother encouraged us to love and respect him. Mommy was virtually stuck with 5 kids and no money, but I never missed a meal, felt unwanted or unloved in any way. Kudos to Mommy!

CHAPTER 8

SARAH'S SMILE

La La La La La La La La La La means I love you.- Delphonics

I met my best friend, Sarah Jane Weeks, while attending John Wanna-maker Jr. High. We skipped school and roamed the streets of Philadelphia, using the subway and elevated rail cars as a speeding playground. We jumped between moving cars, laughing and playing, never giving a second thought to the inherent danger we were in.

What fun we had! We even bought some invisible ink and sprayed it on any poor soul who happened to be wearing white, nurses, cleaning ladies, whomever. They all got hit... frequently. From Sarah Jane, I learned how to skip school and forge absentee letters from unaware parents. I was on top of my game.

Sarah Jane lived with her adopted grandmother at 24th and Diamond, in a newly renovated 3-bedroom duplex. The duplex was small but very well kept, and we always had plenty to eat whenever I spent weekends there, which was fairly often. No annoying greedy brothers, fighting over food or petty arguments about who was eating more than their share of the meal (usually Robert).

Granny, as we called her, was elderly but in relatively good health. She took very good care of us. She cooked fabulous meals that Sarah Jane and I quickly gobbled up without so much as a second thought. Food was always plentiful and readily available. I remember Granny telling us that she had been a cook at a hotel in Tallahassee, FL., which may as well have been a million miles away, because our only point of reference was the crowded streets of Philadelphia.

Sarah Jane's adoption was open, which was informal and quite common between extended families at that time. This type of arrangement was accepted as rather normal for practical purposes (avoiding legal expenses, court costs, etc.) Custody cases were rarely undertaken in court, unless the child was placed in foster care. Foster care was a situation that most families wanted to avoid at all costs.

It often meant that their children were 'lost in the system,' and most parents did not have the resources to pull them out of state custody. Alternatively, children were sent 'down south' or to nearby relatives, who were more financially stable. Back then, we took care of each other. Black folks did not trust the courts, which had proven to be inherently biased and unjust, even to this present day.

Sarah Jane and I were both members of the junior choir at Mt. Olive Baptist Church on Broad Street, which, unfortunately, was just down the street from the Uptown Theater and up the street from the weekly Sunday afternoon dance at Town Hall, hosted by the beloved DJ Butterball (a heavy-set white boy from South Philly).

I forgot how much it cost to get in, maybe $2.00 or $3.00. Of course, we had no problem lying about our age (I think you had to be at least 16); we were only about 13 or 14 at the time. We blew a lot of church offering money buying sodas and chips and 'slow dragging with boys,' most of them much older than we were.

Later, we wound up on a popular locally televised teen dance show called the 'High Lit' show. During the taping, we were right in front of the camera, grinning and fronting, and trying to look cute. For a while, everything was great, until we realized that we could be seen by everyone in Philadelphia, including our parents and church members.

To make matters worse, a local news station picked up the story about the 'shameful disrespectful teenagers', street dancing to the spiritual 'Oh Happy Day'... Guess what clip they aired, over and over, that's right, the one of Sarah Jane and me frantically running out of the studio, hair flying, our hearts pounding, scared we would get caught (we were supposed to be at choir practice).

We had no idea that we were living through the most pivotal time in history, which shaped the nation, the City of Philadelphia, and ultimately ourselves. The truth is that we made history by just being together and loving each other. I wouldn't trade it for the world.

Sarah Jane and I hung out at the Uptown Theatre at Broad and Columbia. One weekend, our favorite group, The Delphonics, was headlining, and of course, we made it our business to be there. After the show, we made a beeline to the backstage door, where we noticed an unattended stretch limousine, and sneaked in the back door. We hid on the floor unnoticed. We didn't know where we were going and didn't really care.

We were in a limousine. The limo drove us to West Philly, about 25 miles from where we lived in North Philly. When we arrived, there was a big party going on. The Delphonics were all in attendance. The adults there didn't really notice us. We were both wearing knee socks and fell asleep on the couch. One of the ladies at the party finally noticed us and asked us where we lived.

She put us in a cab, paid for it, and sent us home. It was about 2:00 in the morning when we finally got home. Mommy was up waiting for us, brandishing a shoe. As soon as we got home, she went to town, striking both of us hard with the shoe. We didn't care; we were still in a daze from the party and being close to the Delphonics.

Looking back, I realize how lucky we were that night. Nobody approached us or offered us alcohol. We wouldn't have known what to do if they did. Sex with minors was strictly forbidden, and everybody knew better than to mess with 'jailbait'. The adults at that party looked out for us, and got us home safe. We were just two young teenagers, looking for fun and adventure. We found it, and somehow made it home in one piece.

We continued to hang out together. Although we were only a few years apart, she was way ahead of me in the game of boys. She also had a nice butt and breasts, not to mention the treasured 'light skin'. Boys would chase me down just to ask me where my 'redbone' friend was. Some said they couldn't tell if it was me or my brother, June, because we looked so similar from behind. Anyway, I had a total crush on one of my brother's friends, Ronald Alston.

Of course, he didn't know I was alive and proceeded to chase after Sarah Jane. One weekend, I found them together, having sex on my brand new Sandra Dee Hollywood bed. They thought nothing of it, but I was heartbroken. I became an expert on Motown heartbreak songs...Seven rooms of gloom, Bernadette...Turn to stone.... Boy, was I sad and rejected. Later, I became very depressed.

Sarah Jane was two years ahead of me in school, so we didn't have any classes together. She seemed to be a fairly good student. However, I'm not sure if her homework and grades were as closely monitored as mine were.I have always been interested in history, law, and politics.

I continued to read everything that I could get my hands on. Through Sarah Jane, I learned to be bolder, to take risks, to not always follow the rules. She showed me a different way of moving through the world, with more confidence, more swagger, more freedom than I'd ever allowed myself. Even when those things got us into trouble, even when Mommy's shoe came down hard on both our behinds, Sarah Jane never seemed to regret a single adventure. And neither did I.

Our bond continued for over 50 years, through marriage, the birth of our children (whom we both named after each other), as well as life's ups and downs. I do not have a memory where Sarah Jane does not exist. Our love for each other is timeless. We will never say goodbye. My friend, I am still here, still standing by. I will hold dear these memories... as I watched our childhood fly...

TIN SOLDIERS

*V*ietnam

Tin soldiers and Nixon's coming, we're finally on our own. This summer I hear the drumming...Four dead in Ohio... Neil Young/ The Isley Brothers

My brother James and Uncle Greg (Mom-Mom's adopted son) had both been drafted to Vietnam. I sent them letters to a P.O. Box in San Francisco, and wondered what the hell that had to do with Vietnam. I had no concept of distance, no further than the raggedy, tight, graffiti-filled streets of Philadelphia that framed my fractured existence. It often crossed my mind that my brother and uncle could very easily become one of the many killed in battle each day.

I became increasingly alarmed as Walter Cronkite counted the number of Americans who died that day. This fueled the feeling of helplessness and despair that gripped the country. The fact that the war was being broadcast nightly on TV made it a deadly, painful reality that no one could ignore.

The news was my main source of information, that and the Philly Daily News, The Inquirer, and the black newspaper, the Phila Tribune. I gobbled up everything I could get my hands on. Since my mother could not read, I was often asked to read newspapers and letters to her, a task I enjoyed.

The student protests were never far behind. At the time, we lived in the 11th and Diamond Street projects, very close to Temple University. I often saw young white kids in the streets. The war in Vietnam had come home to roost.

My brother James had befriended a young Vietnamese boy, about 10 years old. He sent us pictures of himself. Apparently, he had taken this boy under his wing. One Christmas, he asked my mother to send a care package for him. It included of all things several T-shirts and Fruit of the Loom underwear. This kid had never seen or owned a pair of underwear.

I remember that Christmas so well, because we spent many hours in the small kitchen, baking cookies to send along to the troops, who fought alongside my brother James.

Strange thing, both James and my uncle Greg never spoke about what it was like over there. I did find some ghastly pictures of dead Vietnamese soldiers and civilians alike while snooping through James's things when he returned home from the war. I never forgot the images I saw. It brought the story home, in color, straight to my heart, and it frightened me.

Always interested in politics, I joined the World Affairs Club in the 8th grade. It was an after-school program that looked at underdeveloped countries and how foreign aid, like the Red Cross, helped to feed starving people worldwide. The class discussed famine, drought, and the effects of war in far-off places like Africa, Central America, and the Far East.

Of course, we discussed American foreign policy, especially when it came to Vietnam, which was the major headline story in those days. Along with miles and miles of protesters. All the time, virtually everywhere. Most of my classmates were against the war. However, a few students like me had relatives serving overseas and knew firsthand the horrors our soldiers were facing daily.

I heard people say the war was fought to make Vietnam safe for democracy. But the protesters said it was really about money and power, about big companies wanting to control Vietnam's resources. I didn't know who was right, but I knew my brother was over there, and I wanted him home safe.

The fact was that many 3rd world countries faced extreme hunger, and many were homeless due to famine, brought on by civil war and imperialism. Perhaps it was mostly propaganda, but I could not forget the faces of starving Vietnamese people and other 3rd world children.

Actually, it made me grateful that I was born in the US. Seeing people of color facing starvation brought it all up close and personal. Our classmates were asked to contribute to hunger drives in Africa and other far-flung places we'd never heard of. We saw pictures of starving black children and eagerly gave whatever money we had to help them.

Photos, like the ones I saw in my brother's belongings, do not lie. There is a famous newsreel of a young Vietnamese man being executed, shot in the head by a soldier. The footage was in slow motion, so that the viewer had a clear picture of the bullet as it blew this young man's head off. Nothing was off-limits. The war came to us in living color, every day.

I was deeply disappointed when Nixon won the election over Hubert Humphrey. The war was a large component in that election, and things only seemed to get worse when the US bombed Cambodia. But mostly, I just wanted James and Uncle Greg to come home.

Every night, I prayed they would be safe. Every morning, I was relieved when no telegrams came to our door. And when they finally came home, I hugged them so tightly that I thought I'd never let go. I hold those feelings to this day, a fierce love, anchored in the real possibility of loss. A heavy burden for someone so young.

YOU CAN TELL EVERYBODY

---

*M*eeting Jeff

And you can tell everybody that this is your song, it may be quite simple, but now that it's done, I hope you don't mind that I wrote down in words how wonderful life is while you're in the world. – Elton John

Jeff and I met in the neighborhood. By that time, my parents had separated, and we moved from 11th and Diamond to the Spring Garden Street Projects, just a few short miles from downtown Philadelphia.

Due to our large family, we occupied a three-story house, with very few amenities, just bare necessities. True to form, my mom set about making the place clean and comfortable, much like the house we left.

A kind social worker had helped my mother qualify, citing her 4 sons and one daughter, given that she was functionally illiterate. My 2 older brothers, James and Clarence, were both adults by then and did not live with us. James remained in the army after Vietnam and was stationed in Columbus, GA. Clarence had long since married and moved away, but still lived close by. Uncle Greg married his first love, and they quickly began to start their new life together.

I saw Jeff strolling across the wide, well-tended grassy lawns that separated the row of houses in the projects. He walked over to me and introduced himself. His stride was long and confident, and I was immediately attracted to him. He told me that he had recently lost his father and was home on break from boarding school.

He was now enrolled at Roman Catholic High School, a private Catholic School famous for its highly regarded academic achievements, along with 3 of his 4 brothers. I was impressed. He asked for my phone number, and we began talking almost daily. The telephone was monitored closely by my mom (the FBI, as we called her). It was common for her to listen in on our conversations and loudly demand that we hang up the phone immediately. Reminding Jeff that I was only 15 at the time, too young for a boyfriend.

But Jeff was persistent. He would wait for me after school, carrying my books. He made me laugh with his impressions of teachers and his stories about his brothers. He was smart, could talk about books and music, and had dreams of going to college.

Jeff wanted to be an engineer, build bridges. I loved how he talked about the future like it was something real, something he could actually touch.

His mother was rarely home, often working double shifts as an OR nurse. So, there was very little supervision. My mom was still working as a maid, where I'm sure she was grossly underpaid.

Jeff and I would often hang out at his crowded apartment, where we had no privacy (as if we needed it). I met and became friends with all of his 4 brothers. Nice guys, all of them fine as hell. I was especially fond of his brother Ronald "Skip", who was not only a handsome guy, but very soft spoken, shy, and sweet.

We started going on little dates to watch the movies, stopping for ice cream, and gobbling up endless supplies of the world-famous Philly cheese steaks. We'd walk through the neighborhood for hours, just talking. He told me about losing his father, how hard it was when he died.

I told him about my dad's drinking, about the knife, about the blood on my mother's arm. We shared things we didn't talk about with anyone else.

After about six months, we were "going steady "; we were a couple, going steady, Chile. He was my **BOYFRIEND**....Like Cloris Leachman shouted in Young Frankenstein (our favorite movie). My friends were jealous. Sarah Jane said he was a catch. Even my brothers seemed to approve, though they warned him they'd kick his ass if he hurt me.

Jeff gave me a ring it wasn't expensive, just a little silver band from the five and dime, but I wore it like it was a diamond. He wrote me notes and slipped them into my book bag. He walked me home from school every day. He made me feel special, beautiful, and wanted. I felt like I mattered to someone outside my family.

We even held our own marriage ceremony in my mother's kitchen one afternoon when nobody was home. We lit candles, held hands, and made up our own vows. He would tell anyone who would listen that he had married me twice. It was silly, childish, but it felt real to us. We thought we were in love.

Being a stubborn and curious teenager, interested in all that hidden stuff I'd heard about, I was more than willing to explore. I began to sneak over to his house in the apartment development across the street from me, called Penn Towne. We shared our childhood stories and dreamed about our future together.

The subject of sex was a part of many conversations. We'd make out on his couch when his brothers were out, going further each time, testing boundaries. One day, after about a year of dating, when my house was empty, we engaged in my first awkward sexual experience. Nothing to write home about, but we thought we were in love.

We were playing with fire that would soon tear both of our lives apart.

Birth control was not an option back then. Minors could not get it without parental consent, and we were too hot in the pants to even think of using a condom. My high school friends had hipped me to the rhythm method, so I could avoid getting pregnant while I was ovulating.

Best buddy Sarah Jane had given me a month's supply of birth control pills, which were somewhat new at the time.

I took them religiously, not fully understanding how they worked. I did not dare tell my mom; she would have happily killed me if I crossed the line.

Which I did, jumping in headfirst, until my pregnancy thrust me into a world of fear and doubt.

We're so sorry, Uncle Albert, we're so sorry if we caused you any pain, but the kettle is on the boil, and we're so easily called away... Paul McCartney

The Baby....What baby?

Now here I was pregnant at 15 by my darling Jeff, an oversexed, ill-bred, teenage ho. Neither of us had a clue. Apparently, I had put the proverbial "cart before the horse".

I would have a baby before I had an orgasm, learned to drive, graduated from high school, or known the love of a good man. Back in 1971, I was a terrified teenager, hobbled by shame.

I missed my period after sleeping with Jeff, a decision that I deeply and instantly regretted. I went to a local clinic and had a pregnancy test.

They called it the rabbit test. Back then, I don't know why, something about "the rabbit died". They told me to call back in a few days, while I continued to pray for my period. Nothing.

I called the clinic, and the doctor came on the line and said, "Congratulations, you're pregnant."

Maybe he was used to giving that kind of news rather blithely or didn't notice how young I was, but he was very cheerful about the whole thing. Although it wasn't hot outside, I broke out in a James Brown "Cold Sweat". I held the phone tightly. I was in my mother's bedroom, sneaking to make the call. This may as well have been a death sentence.

Afterwards, all I could think of was how hurt my mother would be and how stupid it was to find myself in such an untenable situation. I didn't want her to be ashamed because of something stupid I did. At the time, abortion was illegal, but people still had them. My mother was dead set against abortion, but my situation was different, right?

Suddenly, my dreams of hopping a bus to New York to become a model were lost. My application for the Ms. Black Teenage Beauty Pageant was now voided. The pictures I took for the application were discarded. I slipped into a very deep depression and stopped eating.

To add to my troubles, I took up smoking. (Everybody smoked in those days; I even remember lighting up in the labor room, unheard of now.)

I was ashamed and afraid. Especially to be seen pregnant after Jeff had paraded with his new girlfriend, Cathy, throughout the neighborhood. I heard through the grapevine that she was only 13, and she, too, was pregnant with Jeff's child. Not only that, but Jeff was welcome to sleep with the girl at her house, with her mother's full knowledge and permission.

Later, I would learn that having two women pregnant at the same time was not uncommon, but at the time, it made me feel worthless and discarded, like a fool.

Most young girls were kicked out of school and shunned by the community, and almost always abandoned by their baby's father. Very few stayed around to help raise their offspring. Court-ordered child support was rarely enforced, if it existed at all. For these young girls, their lives took a terrible, predictable turn: welfare, bad housing, the projects, no education, more babies, poverty, despair, and a hard-ass life.

All done within a 10-block square radius, from birth to death, with little variation. Very few people actually made it out of the hood; the few that did never looked back.

Brook later told me what mommy said when he suggested that I go to New York to have an abortion. Mommy said No way, we are a family that gives life, not takes it away". That quote still resonates with me today. Even though I didn't hear it directly, it was pure Mommy.

I knew I had to do something not to bring shame to my mother, who warned me not to "get into trouble". It was early spring, and I certainly didn't want to walk around the neighborhood all summer long with the shameful Scarlet Letter of pregnancy waving like a big red fucking flag (pun intended). Abortion was out of the question.

Later, I called 411 and asked the operator to give me the number to a home for unwed mothers. I heard that such places existed, but I didn't know where they were or what they did. I got the number to the Florence Crittenden Service in Germantown and made an appointment.

At the time, I was in my first year in a pilot program designed for college-bound students at an all-girls high school. I always got good grades and was nominated for the program by my high school counselor. I got in, Mommy was thrilled. All she wanted for me was a good education.

While still a baby, my mother lost both of her parents, who had died young during an epidemic that swept through her small town in Virginia. Miraculously, her young life was spared. Her older sister, Ruth, raised her; Mom never knew her mother or father.

She was denied the chance to go to school and was unable to read or write. She firmly believed that an education was the only way out of poverty; apparently, she was right. My getting pregnant had let her down and disappointed her greatly. I had made a big mess and was filled with hurt, shame, and remorse.

FLORENCE CRITTENDEN

---

*T*he Florence Crittenden Service

Baby, Grandma understands that you really love that man –
Bill Withers

I knew I had to tell Mommy that I was pregnant, but I didn't know how to broach the subject. After obtaining information about a home for unwed mothers, The Florence Crittenden Service, I made an appointment and arranged an interview with Ms. Domanski, the program director. I was trying hard as hell to come up with a plan that would save my skin from mommy's wrath. Not to mention my dad and Mom-mom.

Living in the city had many great advantages: schools, hospitals, and virtually everything was accessible via public transportation. I got directions from the receptionist and made my way to the home. I walked from the bus stop and followed the directions carefully.

The neighborhood looked ritzy, and the streets were lined with beautiful, large oak trees that waved gently in the early summer breeze. The stately houses were made of stone and looked like castles to me. Although I was scared, I pushed on. I was alone.

The Florence Crittenden home was actually a large, converted mansion. It had three stories, with beautifully manicured lawns and lovely flowers growing everywhere. The house boasted a large sunny wrap-around porch. Once I arrived, I was escorted upstairs to Ms. Domanski's office.

I explained my dire circumstances while she sat at her desk and listened quietly, rarely interrupting, often nodding and smiling while encouraging me to tell my story. She asked me about my plans for the baby, and I told her that I wanted to give the child up for adoption.

I was only 15 and had no idea how to take care of a baby. I was scared. More importantly, I had not told my family and desperately needed a way out of this mess. I explained that I was enrolled in a special academic program for college-bound students, and a baby would ruin those plans.

Ms. Domanski showed me around and gave me an application for enrollment into the program. Yes, she could help me, and yes, I could give the baby up for adoption and move on with my life. I filled out the paperwork and felt a tiny spark of hope. Since I was a minor, my mother had to sign over temporary custody of me to Florence Crittenden.

I readily agreed to the plan. I caught the bus back home just brimming with hope. It was later determined that I was almost 3 months pregnant.

The plan was to enter the home in late August, before I started showing and before school started that September. The next morning, I sat down at the kitchen table and told my mother I was pregnant and what I wanted to do about it.

I dreaded that conversation. I consoled my mother as silent tears rolled freely down her dark brown cheeks. It hurt me to see her in such pain. Seeing her so hurt bothered me more than my present circumstances.

About 3 weeks had gone by since I found out I was pregnant, so we had to move fast before I started showing. I had another appointment at Florence Crittenden, but this time my mother was present. Ms. Domanski patiently explained the program and stated that she agreed that I should give the baby up.

The child was innocent and deserved a chance at a good life. I could tell that my mother was reluctant to sign the paperwork, but she did. I moved to Florence Crittenden in late August. I stayed until my baby came in late December.

In the meantime, there was much happening behind the scenes that I wasn't aware of. For instance, this was a privately run home for rich white girls who got into trouble and had to go into hiding, which was a common practice back then. I'd gone to school with whites, but never lived with them.

I found out later that room and board were very expensive. We had a full-time nurse, a cook, and a maid around the clock. Ms. Domanski obtained a scholarship for me so that I could live there at no cost to my financially strapped family. A generous gift, I was lucky to be there, very lucky.

My room was on the top floor with 2 single beds and a dresser. I shared a room with a girl named Betsy. She, too, was scared to death, but we did not become friends. Instead, I bonded with the only other black girl there, named Jody. She was also due in December. She was from West Oak Lane, an exclusive middle-class neighborhood where mostly black professionals lived.

As far as I knew, I was the only person there on a scholarship. Jodi and I hung out every day and supported each other. There was also a rather extensive library, which I took full advantage of. I read Margaret Mitchell (Gone with the Wind), Jane Austen, and a host of other classics. Additionally, there were plenty of gently used maternity clothes, apparently left by former residents. We could go and pick out what we wanted. Cute stuff.

Each girl was assigned a social worker to help guide them through this difficult journey. My social worker was Ms. Weiss. I explained that I was in a special academic program at school and would surely be kicked out once my pregnancy was discovered, which was common practice at the time.

Apparently, pregnant teenagers were a bad influence on other girls, so they were kicked out of school with no recourse. GED did not exist at that time. However, Ms. Weiss, this kind, resourceful young woman, contacted my high school and arranged a private tutor for me, again at no cost.

I think the tutor came about 2 or 3 times a week for lessons to make sure I kept up with my classmates, while I waited for the baby to be born. Additionally, we all had classes on nutrition, homemaking, and, of course, childbirth, which I'll admit I was still terrified about. Didn't some women die from childbirth?

Ms. Weiss and I had many, many talks; her advice was priceless. She assured me that my life was not "ruined" because I got pregnant. "Pregnancy is a natural event, and you have nothing to be ashamed of. After all, you are still a teenager, you can still go to the prom, and attend college, your dreams don't have to die here," Ms. Weiss said. Her advice gave me a new perspective and a little hope.

During my 7th month, I got a job babysitting for a wealthy family who lived in the suburbs. They had a cute little blond-headed boy named Ian. I had to take a commuter train, my first. There, I got my first glimpse of how the other half really lived. Large, beautiful homes with lawns the size of a football field. I was lucky to be able to earn a few dollars. Once again, God was with me as I made plans to give away my child.

There was a phone booth on the second floor, and yes, Mom-mom called often to check on me. She remained a major presence in my life, for which I will always be grateful.

The Catholic Wedding

One of the girls at Florence Crittenden got engaged and decided to marry her child's father. Everyone pitched in to help. We bought inexpensive wedding gifts and supported her decision to marry her child's father.

The wedding was held in a Catholic church, with huge, beautiful stained glass windows. We all crowded in the van and attended the hastily arranged wedding.

I had never been inside a Catholic Church, much less attended a Catholic wedding ceremony. We lined the pews, big stomachs and all. I noticed a set of padded cushions lined neatly on the floor. I soon discovered that they were there for patrons to kneel during prayer. I thought that was strange, but what did I know? During the ceremony, we were required to stand and kneel several times while the priest performed the ceremony and blessed the union. The padding came in handy.

I remember feeling very happy for her. I don't remember her name, but I remember how radiant and happy she looked. This girl had beautiful, long blond hair and wore a simple white dress with a small veil.

After the wedding, we had a little reception in the church basement. Looking back, I realized that she had a "shotgun wedding", but the grace and beauty I witnessed during that wedding were extraordinary. It took a lot of class to host a bunch of unmarried pregnant teenagers at your wedding. Her family was very charming and welcoming, and treated us kindly.

All said it was a very nice, eye-opening experience for me. I couldn't help but notice the cultural and religious differences. We all wished her well as she moved out and began her new life.

ALL THAT GLITTERS, AIN'T GOLD

*H*aving a baby at 16

People make the world go round - The Stylistics

Doctor appointments were bi-weekly until the eighth or ninth month of pregnancy. In the ninth month, we went every week. A little van took us to and from appointments.

We were given wedding rings to wear while on outings, which I refused to wear. I never took one. Fuck it. I didn't want to pretend. This situation was awkward enough without the phony wedding ring.

I was the youngest person at Florence Crittenden. Most of the girls were in their late teens or early twenties. My once small waistline had disappeared, and this large lump began to form in the pit of my stomach. I nicknamed it Lumpy. Sean had that nickname before he was born. Yes, that's what I called him, holding him close and telling him the story of his birth. Of course, I left out the gross parts.

The doctor noticed my weight and was concerned that the child would be born seriously underweight. I had stopped eating.

I was in a deep depression, and nothing could shake it. He ordered an amniocentesis, a procedure that extracts amniotic fluid to determine the size of the baby and find out if the lungs were mature enough for it to breathe on its own.

I was not given any anesthesia so as not to injure the baby. The needle seemed to be about a foot long. The doctor pushed and prodded until the baby was out of harm's way. A nurse squeezed my hand while I gritted my teeth as the needle was inserted into my womb. Yes, it hurt. Badly.

The baby would have to be placed in an incubator if he were under five pounds. I felt it move inside me and became acutely aware that this little person was helpless, with no one to depend on but me. I was determined to see it through. I quit smoking, started eating regularly, and prayed for my child's safe journey to this place we call Earth. Suddenly, it occurred to me that this was bigger than me. I resolved to see my baby come safely into the world.

I began to notice the baby's sleeping patterns when it was awake and when it was asleep. I also knew when the baby was hungry. It tumbled around restlessly until I got something to eat. I began to realize that this was a whole human being, ready to enter the world.

Some of the girls were having their babies and being forced to give them up. While things were slowly changing with respect to unmarried mothers, it was still looked upon as a disgrace. These young women would come back to the home empty-handed, crying and wailing in despair over their lost babies.

My roommate Betsy cried terribly for days until her uptight parents came to get her. We lined up in the hallway to kiss her good-bye. I resolved then to keep my baby. No one could love my child more than I, or so I thought at the time.

Seeing the pain that some of the new mothers were enduring was horrific. Most of them left the babies at the hospital and went straight home, so I didn't get to see what they actually went through—until that day with Betsy. My heart broke for her, and I resolved to keep my baby.

I sat down with Ms. Weiss, and we discussed the possibility of adoption again. I had already signed the papers, relinquishing my rights to the baby.

I asked about what would happen to my baby when he or she was adopted. Would I be able to see my baby or find out how it was doing? Ms. Weiss was honest and direct. She said, "No, the adoption would be sealed, and you would have no further contact with the baby."

Then I asked her what would happen if no one adopted the baby. Ms. Weiss stated that the baby would be placed in foster care, maybe several different homes until he was eighteen. She also told me that the baby had about a fifty percent chance of being raised in a foster home, largely because he was Black, and there was very little demand for Black babies. The risk was very high that he would be raised in foster care. The concept of "open adoptions" simply did not exist back then.

From where I was sitting, it looked like a lose-lose situation to me. White babies were a different story. Childless couples had very few options outside of adoption at that time.

I went straight to the phone booth and called Mom-mom. She agreed to help me gather things for the baby. I called my mother and informed her of my decision. She emphatically stated that I could not bring that baby home. I called my brother Robert, who was newly married, and he and his wife Sheila agreed to let me stay there until I got on my feet. Keeping in mind that I was still just a high school student.

Once that decision was made, I was on the move. I made stuffed toys and decorated receiving blankets for the baby. I also made simple sleeping gowns with tie strings at the bottom. There was a sewing machine at the home, and I put it to good use. Mom-mom had taught me how to sew, and I finally put that skill to good use.

I NEVER COULD HAVE IMAGINED

The Birth Experience

Won't you look down upon me, Jesus, you've got to help me make a stand, my body's aching and my time is at hand. Fire and Rain - James Taylor

After the amniocentesis, my pregnancy moved along without incident. I was at my weekly doctor's appointment when an internal exam revealed that I was dilating. I was three centimeters already and in no pain. The doctor decided that since I was already in the early stages of labor, I should remain at the hospital and have the baby. By then, I was more curious than scared.

Someone at the home called my mother. Mommy and June rushed up to the hospital, which was a considerable distance from where we lived. I breathed a sigh of relief when they entered the labor room. The nurses inserted an IV, my first, and administered medication that would rush me through the labor process, which could last for a few hours to several days. Of course, I wanted to get this over with and looked forward to seeing my child for the first time.

The downside of this method is that it sped up the natural process and forced the baby to come a lot quicker than nature planned. My family was asked to leave. It was late afternoon when I went from regular to hard labor within the hour. The doctor came in with a long, angular instrument and broke my water. The pains came rapidly, nonstop.

The nurses came in frequently to check on me. I was rolling around in the bed in excruciating pain. My body was trembling from the strain. I remember thinking, "So this is what it feels like to die." I prayed hard, asking God to save my life.

It's true about the urge to push. It's strong. I grabbed the bedrails and began to push hard. Nothing was more important to me than getting that baby out. The nurses panicked; the baby's head had crowned. They told me to stop pushing. I ignored them. The urge to push was overwhelming. So, I grunted and pushed with all my might. Come hell or high water, this baby is coming out now.

I remember them wheeling me down the hall to the delivery room at breakneck speed. Once there, I was given some anesthesia, but there was no time left for it to take hold. The baby would come naturally. My legs were strapped to the stirrups, which pissed me off, but I was in too much pain to complain.

I looked at the doctor, a young Indian man, as he aimed his scalpel straight for my vagina. I jumped back, and the doctor looked at me sternly. I later discovered a small incision at the very top of my baby's head. He was cut when I jumped back.

The nurse came over to my left side and began to push down on my stomach, which I hated. I wanted to curse her out or kill her. I was in so much pain. Because I was built so small down there, the doctor performed an episiotomy with no anesthesia, there was no time left. My child's life was hanging in the balance. Hell, I just kept pushing. By then, I was crying, even though I tried to be brave.

The second time the doctor aimed the scalpel, I didn't move. He cut me from stem to stern. The nurse did not stop pushing down on my stomach. Suddenly, the baby came out. He was bloody and crying. They put him on my stomach while they cut the umbilical cord.

"It's a boy," the doctor announced. I remember saying, "Thank you, doctor." He smiled at me and said, "No, thank God." He was right. My son's birth was a miracle.

The afterbirth came out quickly. I was still having contractions and in a great deal of pain. I felt a rush of relief when I heard his little cry, which got louder and louder as the nurses took him down the hall to clean him up. I remember thinking proudly, "Be quiet, son, or you'll wake up the other babies."

I had done the impossible, giving birth to a healthy baby under very difficult circumstances. I was proud of myself, content with my decision to keep the baby. I remained in the delivery room for over an hour while the doctors patiently sewed me back together. I heard one of the nurses say that I had over twenty-two stitches.

Well, that answered my question about how a whole baby could come out of such a small hole. Now I have the answer: cut the mother's guts out, that'll do the trick. That's really what I felt like, gutted.

My mother relented and agreed to let me come home with the baby, who turned out to be an adorable little boy, five pounds seven ounces. He was born at Christmas time. The nurse brought him to me in a little elf outfit, complete with a little elf hat. I was smitten. I fell completely in love with this tiny, helpless little baby boy with the tiny green diaper he had been circumcised.

I named him Sean after my best friend Sarah Jane's nickname. Of course, there was Sean Connery, the incomparable James Bond. I loved the name. I thought it would be fitting for a man of culture, class, and education. Surely this could be the man I would raise my son to become. He would be dashing and handsome, drive a flashy red sports car, and pay for dinner with his gold American Express card.

I was in! How naïve...

HATE KNOWS THAT LOVE IS THE CURE

*F*irst Weeks Home with the Baby

I know you've been hurt, but so have others too, but that's a sacrifice that life puts you through – Bobby Womack

When my mother, brothers, and friends came to see the baby and me, I had hidden Christmas gifts under the bed to surprise them. Ms. Weiss brought them to me when she visited. Robert and Sheila also came. We took pictures. It truly was a festive occasion. The tide had turned. I had a new identity as a mother; it felt spectacular. My mother was beaming. I felt like I'd won the lottery.

I was so happy with the results. Much to my mother's dismay, I slid slowly down the hall and took a shower, unheard of in those days.

My resourceful mother had gotten a neighbor to drive us all home. When I got there, my old bedroom was completely transformed into a nursery. Sean had a white crib complete with a mobile, a changing table, and loads of diapers. The baby clothes I made at Florence Crittenden were brought to my house. Friends and family came bearing gifts, and my mom put on her usual fabulous Christmas dinner.

One of my brothers painted my bedroom a charming light blue. I remember asking, "Suppose it was a girl?" They laughed and shrugged, taking turns holding and feeding the baby. Motherhood felt good.

My mother hovered over the baby constantly. I believe she really got a kick from having a new baby in the house.

I had a nightlight in our room, and she would appear whenever the baby cried. I often cried with him.

You and me against the world, sometimes it feels like you and me against the world...for all the times we cried, just remember that God was on our side. – Helen Reddy

Back to reality

I was scheduled to return to high school in January, in four weeks instead of the usual six. I was happy to be back. A few of my buddies knew about the baby; most didn't. Maybe it was just plain shame, or maybe I just wanted to protect myself from public scrutiny. Nevertheless, I was back in school, where I belonged.

Things were rough at first. I had no babysitter and had to catch two buses in the dead of winter to get to the babysitter, a friend of my mother's. To be honest, I don't know how I did it. Sometimes it rained or snowed, but we trudged on with books, baby, diaper bag, and umbrella when it rained. I remember standing at the bus stop in the rain, freezing cold, crying hard, because the umbrella wouldn't open.

I would be very devoted to my son throughout his life. Unfortunately, and unbeknownst to me, love and devotion alone would not be enough for a poor project girl to raise a boy into a full-grown man. Not to mention the random effects of genes, inherited diseases, family curses, and the like.

It's funny now, but when I look back, I realize that I went from age sixteen to thirty-five virtually overnight. I had skipped the whole damn growing-up thing! It wasn't until years later that I realized that I had handed over my entire youth, without so much as a second thought. Remember that youth is a gift. Treasure it, and use it to your full advantage. It is a blessing. It's fleeting.

Reality had set in. I was in way over my head, and I knew it. It was too late to turn back, and besides, I didn't want to. I was in gym class when the pain started. I was doubled over and had to be helped to the nurse's office. She called an ambulance, and I was rushed to the nearest hospital.

Apparently, I had somehow gotten an infection, possibly because I hadn't fully healed from Sean's birth. I was given antibiotics and was in the hospital for several days. Talk about rough, this was it!

Once back in school, I picked up where I left off. I even got a babysitter who lived across the street. I hit the ground running.

I reunited with my old scholastic competitor and friend, Felicia Renee. She became Sean's godmother. She often took Sean to doctor's appointments so I wouldn't miss exams or deadlines. He was a fragile, sickly child who needed to wear orthopedic leg braces and specially made shoes. At birth, both of his legs were so horribly twisted that he would not be able to stand straight or walk without help.

I remember his first pair of shoes cost about one hundred dollars, which was a fortune back in 1972. In today's money, roughly about four hundred dollars in baby shoes. He needed a new pair every three to six months.

His father happened to see him at the babysitter's and confronted me, asking why "his son" was wearing shoes with the toes cut out. The truth is that false bravado never takes the place of real compassion and genuine concern, which I desperately needed at the time.

My beautiful son was thriving in spite of the odds against him. He was adored by my brothers, who determined that they would make a man out of him by taking him to ball games and lifting him up really high, really fast. I was delighted to be anyone's mother. I felt honored.

Back in the day, a mother was respected and adored. Nowadays, the roles are reversed. Mothers have become equals to their daughters. They are friends. They fail to lead by example. There are no boundaries, no mutual respect. It's a very sad development.

GRADUATION AND MOVING FORWARD

N o Pomp and Circumstance Here

The next year passed quickly as I prepared to graduate from high school without too much drama. I was proud to graduate with my class at age seventeen. My folks stood by me and made sure I didn't miss a step.

And yes, I did go to the prom. My brother, June, and I double-dated. His date was a schoolmate of mine whom I nicknamed Fuzzy. My date was this cute guy I met at a party with a gigantic afro. We drove to New York and stayed in a nice hotel, trying to act like grown-ups. We had a great time.

My son continued to remain sickly. His formative years were rife with frequent trips to the doctors' offices and the dreaded emergency ward. Needless to say, just keeping him alive, clothed, and fed became a daily mission for me. I gave it all I had.

I was fortunate enough to get summer jobs and part-time jobs, some with good companies, like Smith-Kline, a well-respected drug company several blocks away, but still within walking distance from my home. Finally, after graduation, I was offered a job at Travelers Insurance Company. It was my first real job. I was very impressed with myself. I was there for a little over a year.

Unfortunately, I was fired after being absent for several days. Sean was in the hospital again and needed care after he was released. No babysitter, and my mother had to work. Jeff showed up angry and loud, demanding why I didn't tell him that "his son" was in the hospital.

I told him that he did not have a son. I reminded him that he had denied his child and had steadfastly refused to help support him. Sean was about three years old at the time. Jeff slapped me. I hit him back. We fought in the hospital lobby.

Days later, when Sean was about to be released, the hospital demanded an eight-hundred-dollar co-pay before they would let him come home. I paid it in full. My savings evaporated. I had no job, yet I resolved to get back on my feet somehow. I just didn't know exactly how.

Will I Ever Learn?

My mother and I were at each other's throats. Enter fuck-boy, who would uproot me from home and almost derail my entire life. I had taken up with a man in the neighborhood who was notorious for selling drugs. He was twenty-three, I was seventeen. I met him while trying to score a bag of weed.

We became fast friends. It was not long before the grapevine ratted us out. My mother, the Pisces, was furious, determined to save her daughter from God knows what.

She, of course, was right. I was in love/lust. He had introduced me to oral sex. I had my first orgasm. That's right, I had a whole damn human being before I knew what sex was really about. I was hooked. People were stopping me on the street, saying they heard I was seeing him. Why?

Finally, my mother cornered me, and I told her what was going on between us. All of the color left her face as she flopped down in the kitchen chair. "Why didn't you tell me this before? This is dangerous for a girl your age. You can be really taken advantage of, just with that," she said as she pointed to my crotch.

Unfortunately, I did not listen to her and stormed out of her house to be with my drug-dealing boyfriend. Fortunately, this did not last long. He was arrested for, guess what, selling drugs, and I was forced to come back home with my tail tucked between my legs.

Mommy was right. I was a fool. This would not be the only time the universe stepped in to protect me from my stupid mistakes.

My mother and I continued to be at each other's throats, so I moved out. I found an apartment in East Falls, home of Grace Kelly, a.k.a. junkie's paradise. Hoping to get away from my mother's prying eyes and constant demands, I resented her intrusion and did everything in my power to avoid her. I wound up in my apartment alone. The drug dealer boyfriend had been busted for bad checks. I gave up the ghost. I dumped him. Good sex or no good sex, I was outta there.

Fortunately, an old friend introduced me to a homeless fourteen-year-old girl named Joi Jones. She had a young son named Dennis and needed a place to stay. Her uptight Christian parents had kicked her out after she eloped with a neighborhood boy, who then promptly dumped her. We became fast friends and remained so for several years. She took the spare bedroom and set about decorating the dumpy, roach-filled apartment.

I remember waking up in the middle of the night to get some water. Everything was covered — the entire kitchen — covered in nasty squirming brown roaches. They were even on top of each other. It looked like something out of a horror movie. I've seen roaches before, but this was off the chain. I was mortified, screaming and crying.

Joi grabbed me by the shoulders and shook me violently, forcing me to calm down. She reminded me that this was all we had until we could get the hell out of there. We bombed the place. We even tried several home remedies, but nothing really worked. The roaches marched on. I felt trapped, doomed. As usual, Mommy was right. We had to get the hell out of there, and soon.

CHAPTER

16

DREAMS OF TEMPLE UNIVERSITY

C ommunity College of Philadelphia

I'm (Not) Every Woman – Chaka Chan

I did not abandon my dream of going to Temple. When I was a senior in high school, I applied to Temple University. My grades were fair, but not very good. I had taken the SAT and had gotten a fairly decent score, so there was hope, at least from my point of view. The admissions office called me in for an interview.

During the interview, I told the counselor that I was a single mother, and that probably killed it. Instantly, the admissions lady removed her glasses and slammed them down on her desk. She looked at me sharply. I watched as her entire expression changed from polite to curt, to impatient, and finally, just plain old mean. She looked at me sternly and told me that there was no way that I could get into Temple, much less graduate. She rushed me out of her office.

My heart sank. I just watched this so-called "admissions coun-selor" destroy my dreams, and with it my hopes of providing a de-cent life for my son and me. Strangely enough, this event would strengthen my resolve and alter the course and direction of my life. Years later, as a college administrator myself, I would often look back at this incident to remind myself of the power of words and their ability to change the trajectory of one's life.

I remember clutching the school catalog as I ran down the dirty subway stairs at Broad & Columbia Avenue, bitter tears stinging my eyes. I had to get into Temple. I just had to. It was my only way out of the mess that had become my life.

By the time I got home, I felt thoroughly dejected. My roommate, Joi, made some homemade cookies. She had begun to decorate the apartment. She put up a lovely goldfish tank with two colorful Siamese fighting fish and a couple of goldfish. Lovely! I pinched off a few dollars and purchased an old, comfortable rocking chair. I topped it off with a stylish long silver high-arching lamp. I called this my "study corner" and resolved to use it as a jump-off point to get me into Temple.

In the meantime, I decided to go to the Community College of Philadelphia. At the time, it was the only school that would accept my mediocre high school grades. The objective was to get good grades at Community so I would have a crack at getting into Tem-ple.

So I went, every day for two straight years, earning an associate degree with decent grades, in record time.

But I was very lonely then. I had been with ex-boyfriend Jerry Carter in jail, and crazy-ass Jeff was no option. He continued to bed every woman he met while deftly avoiding taking care of his son. Why not? Just like the Royals, he had an heir and a spare.

My son had two brothers. The first, named Jeffrey, arrived a few weeks before Sean was born. The second son, Michael, was born only ten months later. He and Sean looked just alike. I loved Michael for that.

Community College of Philadelphia was the only school that would accept my high school grades. The objective was to get good grades at Community so I would have a crack at getting into Temple. So I went, every day for two straight years, earning an associate degree with decent grades, in record time.

I quickly learned that there was a commuter train that went straight from East Falls to downtown Philadelphia, the location of the Community College. I felt that I was finally beginning to make some real headway towards getting an education. The goal of attending Temple as planned was now within reach. During my freshman year, I took a combination of core classes, psychology, and world history, making sure that the classes were transferable to Temple.

My first class at Community College was World History 101, held in a massive lecture hall that seated about 150 students. I arrived fifteen minutes early, clutching my secondhand textbook and a notebook I'd bought at the dollar store. Most of the other students looked so young, so carefree. They traveled in packs, laughing about parties and weekend plans. I found a seat in the third row, close enough to hear everything, far enough back not to draw attention.

Professor Mendez was a short, energetic man with wild gray hair and an infectious passion for ancient civilizations. Within five minutes of starting his lecture, I was completely absorbed. He didn't just recite dates and facts; he brought history alive.

He paced the front of the room, gesturing wildly as he described the fall of Rome, making us see the chaos, feel the desperation of a crumbling empire.

"History," he said, pausing dramatically, "is not about memorizing names and dates. It's about understanding why people made the choices they did. It's about seeing patterns.

Once you see the patterns, you understand that nothing happening today is really new. It's all happened before, just wearing different clothes."

I wrote down everything he said, word for word. Around me, other students were half-listening, doodling in their notebooks, or whispering to friends. But I was riveted. This was exactly what I'd been hungry for: someone to help me make sense of the world, to give me tools to understand why things were the way they were.

When class ended, I sat there for a moment, watching Professor Mendez gather his papers. I wanted to thank him, to tell him how much that lecture meant to me, but the words stuck in my throat. Besides, he was already surrounded by students asking about the syllabus and exam dates.

Walking out of that lecture hall, I felt something I hadn't felt in a long time: hope. Maybe I really could do this.

I did well in most of my classes, hustling textbooks by day, and studying at night and early morning. At times, my grades suffered; instead of my usual A or B, I was earning C+ and B's. The strain of the long commute, having to study at night, Sean's health, and plain old exhaustion, took its toll on my grades.

I was no longer aiming for an "A", which required much more time and effort than I could afford. Most of the time, I settled for a "C" or a GPA of 2.5 so I would remain eligible for financial aid and transfer to Temple University. I also developed the habit of studying in the college library on Sunday afternoon.

The kids hated it because I'd put together the dreaded "crock pot" for their Sunday dinner. They complained that everything tasted the same. They were probably right, but I wouldn't admit it. I had to keep moving. I kept an oversized appointment book. I would write down any and all pending events. Class assignments, final exams, doctor visits, family occasions, PTA meetings, shopping lists, you name it, I wrote everything down. It was the only way I could keep up with the dizzying amount of 'to-do' lists.

At the time, I probably didn't fully appreciate the fact that I had gained a considerable amount of skills and resources simply by juggling motherhood, high school, and life all at the same time. Transitioning from high school to college was no mean feat.

The work was hard, the academic demands were much more stringent, but I had a point to prove, mainly to myself if no one else. I leaned heavily upon my experience as a teenage mother, and it helped to sharpen the skills I needed to meet the demands of college life.

I remember during college orientation, at Temple, the Dean of Students stood up and made quite a little speech. Before he sat down, he said, look to the left, now look to the right. One of you will not be here next semester.

The statement hit home as I realized the gravity of my situation. I slid further down in my seat. The old fears quickly crept in to haunt me...those kids have more than you... They went to private school... they have parents... they don't have babies...you'll never make it.

Nevertheless, I developed good study habits, obviously, so I could pass the exams. Sometimes the teachers would state, "This will be on the exam." Duh. I would write down the lecture points word for word. Often, I would reverse concepts in the textbooks and ask the teacher to clarify the meaning after class. I made sure I understood the course objectives, ensuring at least a passing grade.

Of course, I would first make sure I understood the material, highlighted it in the textbook, and then reframe it in a reasonably intelligent manner, just to make sure I fully understood the content. The no-brainer was turning in classwork on time, taking good notes, and acing the exams. I would write in the margins of the textbooks (if I owned them) and highlight the text that I believed the professor was using to illustrate his point.

Often, the final exams would be the little 10-page blue booklet. The teacher would write one comprehensive question on the board. There were no true or false or multiple-choice questions. Yes, you had to write all 10 pages, no skipping. You either knew the material and could explain it, or you flunked the class.

This kind of final exam was wholly dreaded among my peers, me included. Open-book exams were unheard of! The student who finished first stood up and proudly strolled out of class, and was looked upon as a genius.

I began to notice a rather interesting phenomenon: all the smart kids sat together and formed study groups, etc. I also noticed that the students who weren't really committed for one reason or another either dropped the class or simply disappeared. There is some truth to the fact that you are a reflection of who you hang around with. No need to guess which group I hung out with.

It was during my second semester that I really connected with a study group in my psychology class. There were five of us: me,

Karen, a blonde girl from the suburbs who wanted to be a therapist, Tracy Johnson, a communications major, who would later achieve high honors in her chosen field in the media.

There was Lisa, a loud, funny Italian girl from South Philly, and of course, a Jewish guy who asked a million questions in class. We'd been meeting at the library for weeks, preparing for midterms.

Because I had a house, a few study groups met at my home. We bonded at my house and had a great time listening to music, while we laughed and joked and learned from each other. Someone would bring over a cheap bottle of wine, and we would sit around my living room, study the material, and try like hell to prepare for the mid-term or final exams.

My children slept soundly in their bedrooms during these study groups. It was great fun. I have fond memories of those school days.

Teachers are human beings. In-person class lectures are essential in capturing concepts that were not necessarily understood on a computer screen or piece of paper, where there is little room for interaction and light bulb moments.

Teachers noticed if a student had a genuine interest in the subject or was just there to get an easy grade. Showing up late for class or interrupting a lecture was a definite no-no.

I always made a point of getting to class early, and connecting with the instructor if only to summarize the material and discuss the class objectives briefly after class. I purposely stood out because I wanted to establish myself as a committed student, and I often needed the extra help to fully comprehend the material.

One professor in particular changed the way I saw myself. Dr. Jackson taught Introduction to Sociology at the Community College. She was a tall, elegant Black woman in her fifties who wore colorful African-print wraps and had the most commanding presence I'd ever seen. She didn't tolerate nonsense in her classroom, but she also had this way of making you feel seen.

About halfway through the semester, she assigned a paper on social stratification. We were supposed to analyze how economic class affected educational opportunities. I wrote about my own experience, how being poor and pregnant at fifteen had nearly derailed my education, how the system was set up in ways that made it almost impossible for girls like me to succeed.

I poured everything into that paper: my anger, my determination, my observations about how the women at Florence Crittenden were treated by the outside world because they had made the mistake of getting pregnant without marriage.

When Dr. Jackson handed back the papers, mine had an A+ at the top. But more than that, she'd written in red pen: "See me during office hours. This is important."

My stomach dropped. Had I said too much? Was I in trouble?

I showed up at her office the next day, nervously clutching my backpack. Dr. Jackson looked up from her desk and smiled. "Sit down, Janet. You're not in trouble. Quite the opposite."

She held up my paper. "This," she said, "is the best student work I've read in five years of teaching this course. You didn't just regurgitate theory, you lived it, analyzed it, and drew connections that most of my graduate students can't make." I didn't know what to say. No one had ever talked to me like this before. "Tell me about yourself," she said, leaning back in her chair. "What's your story?"

So I told her. About getting pregnant at fifteen, about Florence Crittenden, about raising Sean and Saida on my own while trying to finish high school, and now college. Dr. Jackson listened without interrupting. When I finished, she was quiet for a moment. Then she said, "Do you know what you have that most of my students don't? You have lived experience. You have survived systems that were designed to break you. And not only did you survive, but you're thriving. You're analyzing those same systems with a clarity that most scholars spend decades trying to achieve."

She leaned forward. "Janet, I don't say this lightly. You need to go to law school. Not social work, not counseling. Law.

Because the problems you've identified in that paper, they're not going to be solved by individual casework. They're going to be solved by people who understand the system from the inside and have the power to change it."

I was stunned. Law school? That seemed impossible. That was for rich kids, for people with connections. Not for single mothers from the projects. "I can't afford law school," I said quietly. "I can barely afford Community College."

"There are scholarships. There are programs for non-traditional students. There are ways." She pulled out a piece of paper and started writing. "First, you need to get into Temple as you've planned. Then you maintain a strong GPA. I'm going to write you a letter of recommendation that will open doors. But you have to believe you can do this."

I left her office that day with something I'd never had before: someone with credentials, with authority, telling me I was capable of more than I'd ever imagined. Dr. Jackson's words echoed Ms. Weiss's encouragement from years before, but now I was old enough, experienced enough, to really hear them.

Most teachers had office hours once or twice a week. Students could make appointments or just show up. Many teachers made it clear about the "open door policy", and encouraged students to stop by with any questions.

Not all teachers necessarily shared this position, and students were not really welcome to come to their office hours, especially if you were an upperclassman, the assumption being that you should know what the hell was going on by then.

Most tenured professors had published books or articles in academic periodicals. Their published works were used extensively in class, so there was little room for free-wheeling interpretation of the text. For me, no grade was easy. I could not afford to fail. Failure would mean that I would lose my financial aid, all my dreams down the drain. Not an option.

Statistics Class - Calculus

As an upperclassman, I had avoided taking any math classes because I simply could not grasp the material. In fact, I had to attend summer school in 10th grade just to pass algebra, which made no sense to me and looked like a huge waste of time; besides, it simply served no practical purpose as I saw it then. I wound up taking a statistics class, which, according to the syllabus, had the dreaded calculus component.

The verdict was in. Without calculus, I could not graduate. As an upperclassman, it was just about the only course I could take without first meeting a math prerequisite (which I did not have). Given that I was technically a transfer student, I made it a point to meet with my academic advisor before and after each new quarter.

Finally, I learned that I had to take a math class in order to meet the graduation requirement. I needed to make sure I stayed on track.

This appeared to be a roadblock for sure. I was stuck. It was now or never. I had inadvertently painted myself into an academic corner. This was the ultimate test. How badly did I want this? What lengths would I need to go through in order to make the grade?

However, once applied, calculus taught me how to think within a specified paradigm and make it understandable. It taught me how to use calculus in critical thinking and problem solving, an essential skill.

I had heard many horror stories of students who dropped out in their senior year or were kicked out for not meeting the academic requirements needed to graduate. I didn't want to be one of them. Previously, I had navigated some pretty treacherous waters and had no choice but to forge ahead, which I did. Fortunately, the math instructor was very generous with his time.

I came to almost every early office hour to review the text and create the statistical report/paper needed to pass the class. This included a statement of statistical facts and the data necessary to support the thesis. In short, you had to create the problem, summarize it within the framework provided, and place it into the formula that supported your thesis. Yes, it literally had to line up, using the formulas provided in the textbook and lecture.

Imagine my delight when I passed the class with a "B". I was shocked. This class taught me a very valuable lesson: you can do anything if you're willing to stretch yourself and give it 'all you've got'. It was the proven (hard) road to success.

I used this acquired skill many times in the working world. Analyzing problems, decoding the answer, and providing a solution. In short, thinking "outside of the box". Trust your intuition and feel free to turn the problem upside down or even sideways like a Rubik's Cube. Be willing to do any and everything to find information to support your thesis and then go for it. You can't go wrong. You will not fail.

Years later, I would find myself advocating for them, protecting them from their mothers' indifference and their fathers' wrath. Both were forced to come to terms with the fact that they brought children into the world under difficult and dire circumstances. They both failed to provide them with the basics, warm clothes, food, and a healthy environment. As a result, Jeff and I held birthday and Christmas celebrations at my house on Wagner Ave, much to their delight.

The children often asked why they had to go back to Cathy, who was indifferent at best. She and their father, Jeff, who seemed to have lost interest in caring for them, had both moved on to greener pastures, so I did what I could to help.

I felt strongly that the children were innocent and did not deserve to suffer because of their parents' poor decisions. They often arrived at my house poorly dressed in freezing temperatures and often hungry or simply underfed.

There were good times, sandwiched between the struggles. One summer, I sent all three brothers to summer camp, and they had a ball. The boys told me that it was one of their favorite childhood memories. I was proud to be a part of that experience for them.

IT'S GREAT UNTIL IT'S NOT

The Ballad of William Talley

Chickens Come Home to Roost - Malcolm X

I was disgusted and still heartbroken over the stupid predicament I found myself in. I had to accept that I would never have the close-knit family circle that I grew up with and longed for. I craved stability and grabbed at anything that looked like a way out.

It was in this desperate, weakened state that I met my husband, William E. Talley, or Billy, as he liked to be called.

He was my roommate's next-door neighbor and awfully sweet, a lot of fun. We dated for two years before deciding to marry. He adored Sean, and I thought we might have a crack at a decent life. We both wanted the same things: a nice house in a great neighborhood, a good education for the kids, the American dream, the good life.

Billy was jovial and kind. He would hold me tight late at night when we would quietly lie close together, talking about our dreams for the future and the wonderful life we would surely have if we just kept pushing and stayed on the right path.

His kindness was the key to my recovery from too much heartbreak, too young. He became the much-needed salve that softened my broken heart and gave me hope for a strong, happy future. East Falls was literally falling apart right in front of us. We were strongly motivated to get the hell out of there.

Eventually, we decided to hurry down to the courthouse and say our marriage vows, without telling anyone. I remember the judge who married us lent me her ring, because we didn't even have one. A gracious gesture that I shall never forget. We're married. Now all we had to do was prepare for the future. We would be set.

Finding a Home

Afterwards, we set about looking for a house. I was purposely being methodical, not emotional, or winging it. I planned every move. In the meantime, the project apartment was quickly being torn down. The elevator never worked. Luckily, we were on the fourth floor, thank God. Of course, the stairwells were never lit, and yes, the junkie part was true.

We often had to step over them in the stairwells while taking the children to day care or shopping. East Falls was situated among the tall spruces along the Schuylkill River, now Kelly Drive. It was a nightmare place to live. Due to the ever-present roaches and fenced-in vistas, it was the true home of criminals, thieves, and malcontents.

Everywhere around us, there was poverty, theft, despair, and deceit. I was determined that my little boy would not be raised in that environment. I immediately stopped paying rent as I struggled to save money for a deposit or down payment, as it turned out. After looking for several weeks, I found a listing for a house in the Logan section of the city. The house on Wagner Avenue was just what the doctor ordered. It had three bedrooms, a full basement, and even a garage, a great place for Sean and my roommate Joi's son Dennis to play and grow up. I was only twenty years old.

I got a small refund from my school's tuition and used the money to put a down payment on the house on Wagner Avenue. The house was under a new program sponsored by the federal government called the FHA, which is still in existence today. This program was one of many housing programs launched in the seventies, designed for first-time buyers. The program prohibited the practice of redlining, which was notorious for keeping Blacks out of white neighborhoods. We applied and were approved for a loan of ten thousand dollars. This program worked in conjunction with other local programs, like OIC, spearheaded by Dr. Leon Sullivan.

This program provided jobs and training for anybody who needed it and helped lift many people out of poverty.

There were many other "poverty programs" introduced during the Johnson administration and further expanded under subsequent administrations. Each program was designed to march against the "War on Poverty" and give every American the right to decent housing and an unobstructed path to home ownership. Of course, in order to apply, you had to have your act together, which meant being married and having a steady income. I felt optimistic about my future for the first time since becoming a mother. I remember signing a waiver stating that Sean did not belong to my husband, Billy. To this day, I don't know why, inheritance, title?

We moved next door to a racist Jewish family, the Resnicks, who immediately put their house up for sale. We didn't give a fuck. I loved the house. It was semi-detached, and the rooms were large and airy. It had plenty of windows, which gave the house a constant supply of natural light. FHA had strict compliance rules, ensuring that the properties met all the current health codes, like removing lead paint, which had recently proved to be dangerous.

All of the appliances were new. The stove and refrigerator, too. I purchased a new washer and dryer from a local furniture store. I added several large houseplants, which really brightened up the place. Joi, who was very talented and artistic, set about decorating and furnishing the house.

We bought twin captains' beds for the boys and put them in the middle room, conveniently decorated with new blue wallpaper. Joi took the large back bedroom. I took the front bedroom. We were all set. We were on a roll.

Billy immediately lost his job. I was furious. Shortly thereafter, I found out I was pregnant. Now that I was married, we agreed I should stop taking the pill, but now I was having second thoughts. We had planned this baby, and now I felt like I had been conned into getting pregnant.

The Franklin Institute

After we moved into the house, I got a coveted summer job at The Franklin Institute as a tour guide. I remembered going there several times as a child. I marveled at the Planetarium, where the famous Kite and Key experiment was showcased. Benjamin Franklin was a hero of mine. I read Poor Richard's Almanac in grade school, which was full of his insightful quotes that still resonate with me today. His contributions to America's quest for independence, his skillful representation of America on the world stage, and his curiosity as an inventor made him a pivotal central character in US history.

The truth is, scratch any Philadelphian, and you will find a wealth of knowledge and history. It's in our blood. We grew up with Betsy Ross and the Liberty Bell. Unlike New York and other busy metropolises, there remain many well-preserved, ground-level historical places in Old City Philadelphia that you can just walk up to. Pennsylvania is known as the Quaker State, due to its settlement of Quakers, who did not support slavery. It became the seat of the abolitionist movement. I am very proud to be from there. Nowadays, these sacred places are carefully guarded, as they should be.

I was indeed pregnant, which proved to be an even greater challenge than the first pregnancy. I remember going to see the gynecologist and him saying I could have an abortion. I declined, rushing out of his office, fearful for my baby's life. Once again, I was in a life-and-death struggle against terrible odds. I was on my own, with a mortgage and plenty of school debt. I kept my cherished job at the Franklin Institute for several more weeks, until the smell of the McDonald's downstairs made me throw up daily.

I retreated to my house on Wagner Avenue and prepared for the new baby. Money was tight, so I spent the fall hunting for bargains in old antique shops along Germantown Avenue. I bought used baby clothes and refinished wooden baby furniture, painting everything white. I also bought a huge bentwood rocker and planned for the birth of my second child. I prayed it was a girl.

BE STILL MY HEART

Billy's Betrayal

During this time, I became aware that my unemployed husband was sneaking around on me. Evidently, he had met up with some chick in South Philly and promised her a house, too. Never mind the fact that he contributed nothing to the down payment or made mortgage payments.

I was his wife, not his mother. Apparently, he did not understand the difference between the two. I fully expected him to work and contribute to the family. Instead, Joi and I kept everything going because we had to. Billy began to stay in South Philly while I struggled with all the responsibilities alone.

I felt trapped, fearfully wondering how I could be so stupid as to let this happen to me again. I internalized this as rejection, rather than seeing it as yet another unfortunate event, another bad decision. I took it as if something was intrinsically wrong with me.

I was unlovable, not good enough, unworthy of being cared for, abandoned by a husband who swore to love and protect me.

Sadly, he left me at my weakest point. By then, I was almost six months pregnant. Once again, I made a solemn vow to protect my little baby. I had to see it through. Depression and despair became my constant companions.

Fortunately, I had a small refund check that would help shield my little family during the coming hard, cold, snowy Philadelphia winter that I was now facing.

The refund check had been mailed to Sarah Jane's address, where I knew it would be kept safe.

However, after several weeks of delays, I contacted the accounting office at school to try to track it down. I called them several times until I got someone on the phone who was sympathetic and offered to look it up. I waited breathlessly for several minutes. When the clerk came back to the phone, she stated that the check had been cashed.

I offered to come down to straighten the matter out. Imagine my surprise when I recognized my best friend Sarah Jane's handwriting endorsing my name on the back of the check. I was livid. Of course, I confronted her, but she said she needed the money.

She lied to me several times, saying repeatedly that the check had not come, while all the time knowing that she had cashed it.

I let it go. Besides, she was living with a man she loved. She would be fine. She promised to pay me back. Later, that same man put her and her children (one of them his) out of HIS HOUSE. They all came and stayed with me for a while. By that time, I had put it all behind me. After all, she was my best friend.

Birth of the baby girl

When I first saw you, I said Ooh My Ooh My... there goes my dream – From Dreamgirls, the play

Although the baby was due in December, she didn't come until January 16th, the same date as my brother June's beloved daughter, Amoy. I was delighted. Billy had been at my house that day and left to go back to his woman in South Philly. I was alone. My water broke, and I called my mother. I woke up Sean and took him next door (the house had since been sold to a young Black couple). I told Mommy I was fine, but she called the police anyway. They rushed me to the hospital. It was a Saturday night.

Here I was yet again, alone, fighting to bring this baby into the world, alone. I had decided to get my tubes tied before she was born. Back then, you needed your husband's permission to tie your tubes. I did indeed forge my husband's signature. I was only twenty-one years old at the time. I didn't tell anyone because I didn't want any pushback. I had been burned twice. I wanted to make sure this misfortune did not happen to me again.

After a very hard labor, the nurse took me back to my room, where I cried bitterly the entire time I was there. The next morning, they brought her to me. Although my heart was broken, I welcomed my little five-pound baby. She had the biggest, prettiest eyes I had ever seen, precious to me. Her name was chosen by her godmother Felicia, a.k.a. Aunt Lee. She had an Arabic name, "Saida Aisha," meaning God's gracious gift.

I had high hopes for my little girl. I prayed that she would grow up wholesome and happy and not make the stupid mistakes I had made. Looking back, my objective was unrealistic. She would need both mother and father, and some goddamn stability, both of which were in very short supply.

My mom came home with me for the first few days out of the hospital. I told her about the tubal ligation. Of course, she vehemently disapproved. Her generation championed a large family. "Be fruitful and multiply." That edict set every woman back a thousand years and subjugated us to a lifetime of being trapped by our bodies. The women's movement was big then.

Women should have the right to determine what happens to their own bodies. Few Black men or white men, for that matter, actually supported their families, and court-ordered child support either did not exist or was not enforced. All across America, women were demanding structural support for their families. After all, we had to work, and someone had to raise the kids while we were out making a living. The issue of education and day care became essential. There would be no way that I could support my little family without an education. I just had to finish college. I was in a fight for survival on several fronts, all at once.

After Mommy left, I tried to settle in and take care of my babies, but something was off. I just could not get my footing, and the baby cried nonstop, perhaps mirroring my sadness and grief. I had slipped into postpartum depression, unheard of at the time. I remained undiagnosed. When Saida was about four weeks old, there was a terrible blizzard. All transportation had stopped. We had an oil heater, which had run dry. The kids and I were trapped in the house, in the dead of winter, in a blizzard, with no heat. I was terrified. I called my mother in a panic.

Somehow, she managed to come to my aid, picking up the kids and me and bringing us through the blizzard to safety at her home. My heart was full of gratitude and still is today. She would step in many times to love and protect my children and me. Her bravery and strength served to define me, as I grappled with the harsh realities of the life I had chosen.

A week later, the snow was gone, and we went back to my house. I finally got the heat back on. God knows where I got the money to pay for a tank of heating oil. I think I wrote them a bad check. I remember thinking that this was dangerous, and I needed to switch to gas heat, and fast. I eagerly turned up the heat. Immediately, hot steaming water came rushing out of the living room ceiling.

We huddled in my bedroom with a space heater. I called my dad, who said I had a busted pipe. I needed a plumber. I didn't know any. I had heard that a neighbor down the street was a plumber. I knocked on his door and pleaded with him to help me. It was nighttime, but he came and fixed the pipe. I had a few dollars in my savings account, which I used to pay the plumber. Now I was flat broke, during a blizzard, with a crying infant, and off to a very shaky start in my new home.

A Word About the Women's Liberation Movement

As I recounted, either by law or custom, most doctors required a husband's permission to get birth control pills or have a tubal ligation, and prior to 1972, abortions were illegal. Women did not control their own bodies, the assumption being that a woman's body was not her own. Along came Gloria Steinem, Fannie Lou Hamer, Shirley Chisholm—the first Black woman to run for president, and many others. Who demanded that the assumption be finally put to rest. Incidentally, women had only recently won the right to vote in 1920.

When Billie Jean King whipped Bobby Riggs's ass in 1973, I was elated. She and Elton John were part of a tennis tour called Philly Freedom. I went to an event they sponsored in downtown Philly and knew that I was a witness to history. I was so proud that she beat the shit out of that loudmouth Bobby Riggs. I felt like I had won the match. I welcomed the women's movement.

I saw how hard my mother's life had become, constantly struggling to feed her large family. Daddy was gone. She was stuck working for scraps for white folks. More babies were out of the question, not likely. You motherfuckers must be crazy! I had seen the light. I wanted no part of this hardship, I declared.

Joi had moved into her own apartment nearby several weeks earlier, and I was indeed alone with the children. As usual, I was determined to make a go of it. The city had a home-based day care program that had a very long waiting list. On a gamble, I signed up for the program while I was still pregnant with Saida. I was delighted to receive a letter early that spring, indicating that I was accepted. The day care lady's name was

TAKING CONTROL

I had recently graduated from Community College and was admitted to Temple in the fall term of 1977, the same year Saida was born. This gave me the opportunity to attend my dream school, Temple University. Once again, the stars aligned to make a path for me. I was overjoyed.

I used the summer to get in shape. My dear friend and aunt by marriage, Donna Pinkney, joined me on our early morning runs. She and my uncle Greg were going through a divorce.

Her gentle kindness helped me through some very rough times. This was before the Walkman, so we gave each other support while we were both catching hell in our personal lives. I gained over fifty pounds during my pregnancy. I also still suffered from postpartum depression and low self-esteem, having to face life as a single mother of two children.

My husband was out of the house, having decided to live full-time with his paramour in South Philly. I guess it beats sneaking around on your wife. No matter how you looked at it, there I was, trapped with two innocent babies and no help in sight. How in God's name did I allow this shit to happen to me twice? Inconceivable. I thought I had more sense than that, apparently not! After all was said and done, I did this to myself. Guess who I was angry with? Self. This pathology affects millions of women all over the world, but at the time, all I could see was what was directly in front of me. Not a pretty picture.

Over those last few years, I had learned to confide deeply in my mother. I found that while she didn't always agree with me, she gave great advice and knew every trick in the book. I readily took advantage of her multi-layered, step-by-step advice. It worked like a charm. Always. One hundred percent of the time.

Billy's Deception Exposed

I was fast asleep when my brother, June, called and asked where Saida was. Alarmed, I jumped up and ran to her crib, where she was sound asleep. June said he had just seen Saida with Billy and a lady. What the fuck? This information hit me squarely in the gut and sent me spinning further down the well of depression. Why wasn't I good enough?

The next morning, I called Mommy, my partner in crime and resident guru. I explained what June told me, and she helped me to clarify some salient points. First, I was no longer pregnant, she said, and besides, turnabout is certainly fair play. "Remember, that's your husband, not hers. That's your house. Run it the way you want to. Play your position. Let's go. By the way, by all means, keep your mouth shut. Now that you have the goods, you can outmaneuver him." Really. How? I will always remember her soft, deep chuckle when she said, "First, get a lawyer."

I did just that. I hired a brilliant lawyer, Mr. Cohen, who was a Temple grad no less. I remember that his office was in the PSFS bank building on Market Street. I held an account at this bank since I was about eight years old, so I felt quite comfortable sitting in his office while he took notes on my divorce complaint. Back then, you needed to "show cause" for infidelity, etc., to obtain a divorce.

There was no such thing as a no-fault divorce. You had to tell the court why you were seeking a divorce. Mr. Cohen did not use the infidelity route. Instead, we chose a clean route, quick and dirty.

When it was all said and done, I got custody of both children and the title to the house on Wagner Avenue.

He was not happy to sign over co-ownership to the house, although he never paid a dime towards the house note and had effectively abandoned his family for what he thought were greener pastures. Of course, he never paid the court-ordered child support. Nevertheless, all is fair in love and war. Was I ready to move forward? Hell yes. But first, a little payback, compliments of Mommy.

Turning the Tables

She reminded me that Billy was still my husband until the divorce was final. It took well over six months, so why not turn the tables a little bit? After all, what's good for the goose—or was it the gander? I forget. My husband was well-endowed, which I'm sure helped to open many doors for him, including mine. Yet I digress. I began seducing my husband every Friday night, which coincidentally turned out to be his payday.

He was supposed to be visiting his new baby daughter. Instead, he visited me. I made sure there was plenty of food, weed, and wine on hand as I repeatedly invited him into my bed. The weight was coming off quickly. I had undergone a tubal ligation directly after my daughter's birth, so there was no chance of my getting pregnant.

My actions were more intellectual than vengeful. I wanted him to know and understand that he had been beaten at his own game, both he and his side piece, with a well-delivered single slingshot, like David and Goliath. He was none the wiser that the tables had been turned against him, not with lies and betrayal, but with true grit and determination.

Yes, my actions were perfectly timed, and I got the exact result I wanted. As his wife, I had to endure pregnancy and childbirth alone and felt thoroughly victimized by those circumstances. His deception was quite evident and undeniable. I no longer felt like a victim, but a strong woman who stood her ground and won. I felt vindicated, victorious. One for the home team.

This blow was for the thousands of women worldwide who bravely endured and beat the odds against them, giving birth to healthy babies under such terrible circumstances. I had faced similar challenges twice, much to my chagrin. I was still standing tall, with my innocent, beautiful babies in tow.

No woman should be made to feel victimized by her own husband while bringing his children into the world. Still today, many fathers simply just walk away, Scott-free, never looking back to face the awful pain they've caused in their children's lives. Thereafter, I gladly took my power back and loved it.

Billy got what he deserved, and I was glad to deliver it. I never regretted my actions. In fact, I was quite pleased with myself. The gig was up, or the proverbial "cat was out of the bag." Karma is a bitch".

There has never been an acceptable excuse for abandoning one's family. Even if you die, life insurance is designed to protect your family. No excuses. None.

I fucked him with wild abandon. No arguments, no complaints. I made sure he was exhausted by the time he took his sorry ass back to South Philly, broke. I sent Sean down south to Georgia to spend the summer with my big brother James, so it was just the baby and me until school started in September. Yes, I got a big kick out of knowing that I was ruffling feathers back in the South Philly ghetto. Here you go, bitch, this Bud's for you.

It was months before they knew what was really going on. Who was really on the take? In the interim, I received a call from a local bank inquiring about a loan against my income tax return. Apparently, Billy and the paramour had forged IRS documents and were about to steal my income tax return.

Somehow, the bank got my telephone number and called to follow up. Of course, I declined the loan, filed my taxes, and got the full refund. I used the money to buy storm windows and prepare the house for the harsh, cold Philadelphia winter ahead. I learned my lesson from the previous year.

Following my mother's advice, I said nothing. "Ease your head out of the lion's mouth," she'd say. So I kept silent about my discovery. They had a baby girl who was only a few months younger than my child. How could this treachery happen twice?

Believe it or not, this situation happens a lot. Nobody talks about the pain and humiliation of having another woman blatantly carry and produce a "whole baby" while married to you. I heard the child's name was Duet, but that is all I know. My daughter could have a thousand brothers and sisters.

She would have to do a deep DNA dive to unravel this mess. She was innocent. I felt we both deserved better.

The Final Confrontation

One morning, after Billy had stayed yet another Friday night at my house, the telephone rang. It was the South Philly paramour, wondering where MY husband was. I politely informed her that MY HUSBAND was lying right beside me, where he was every Friday night. What?

I handed him the phone, smiled sweetly, and told him to get the fuck out of my house. We fought. He won, punching and hitting me repeatedly. I defended myself the best I could. The gig was up. I saw him only once after that incident. He promised to support his daughter and pay for her education. Of course, that never happened. She was only five months old. He never reappeared again to inquire about his daughters' welfare.

FORWARD ALWAYS, ALWAYS FORWARD

G one baby Gone

Days turned into weeks, and weeks into months. Life kept throwing punches, and I kept dodging them, trying to stay standing. Billy's absence became the norm, and I tried to convince myself that I was better off without him. He promised me the world, but he couldn't even give me a steady roof over our heads. I realized, somewhere along the way, that I was done with his empty promises. Done waiting for someone else to save me. I had two kids who needed me, and I couldn't afford to keep wasting my energy on someone who didn't care.

Childcare Struggles

Joi had moved into her own apartment nearby several weeks earlier, and I was indeed alone with the children. As usual, I was determined to make a go of it. The city had a home-based day care program in my new neighborhood on Wagner Avenue. Unfortunately, they had a very long waiting list. On a gamble, I signed up for the program while I was still pregnant with Saida. I was delighted to receive a letter early that spring indicating that I was accepted. The day care lady's name was Ms. Beck, an aging widow who lived nearby with a terrible attitude.

Under the circumstances, I had little choice but to leave my precious baby with Ms. Beck. Saida cried a lot, and I understood that she was hard to deal with. I kept the children home during school breaks and between classes to limit their exposure to her. In the meantime, a few weeks later, I had dropped out of school to take care of my mother anyway, so I didn't need daycare every day, at least for the time being.

Fortune again smiled down upon me when a neighbor opened up a little day care two doors down from me. By then, Saida could walk and talk a little, so I removed my children from Ms. Beck and took them to my neighbor. I didn't leave my children with Ms. Beck for very long, maybe eight or nine months, maybe less. She had a bad attitude, so I simply moved my kids away from her. Problem solved. In short, I fired her.

Pushing Through Exhaustion

I finished Community College shortly after Saida was born, pushing through night classes while working whatever jobs I could find during the day. I wanted more than anything to create a future for Sean and Saida that wasn't weighed down by poverty and instability. I wanted them to see a mother who didn't quit, who didn't let life's setbacks keep her down.

Some nights, I'd come home exhausted, my eyes burning from lack of sleep, my body aching from standing on my feet all day.

But I'd peek in on my kids, sleeping soundly, and I'd know it was worth it. Every sacrifice, every sleepless night. Jeff was around then, and often baby sat the kids while I attended night school during my last semester at Community College.

My daily struggle became a way of life for me. Simple things like holidays, reading the Sunday papers, or going to the park became special events for me. They offered me a respite from the nonstop effort it took to keep my family together. Necessity is the mother of invention, and I still carry the same dogmatic attitude that I had in my youth. Some say this probably landed me in the hospital, but I could not, would not slow down.

I owed it to my people, my ancestors who braved God knows what atrocities to make it in these United States. Exhaustion was simply a by-product of my constant efforts. If I got tired, I ignored it and kept going.

Exhaustion was a luxury I could not afford. I drove myself pretty hard and gave it my all. I had no choice. I had no regrets. My struggles came straight from my heart, out of love for my family, especially my brothers. Love is a great motivator. Yes, I would do it all again without hesitation. It all came out of love.

We keep going because we have to. Because our kids are watching, and they deserve to see a mom who doesn't quit, who doesn't give up, no matter how hard it gets. And that's what I was going to be. For Sean. For Saida. For me.

 After all that, I was still standing. Bruised, but standing. I learned that strength doesn't always look like power; sometimes it's just survival. Sometimes it's holding your baby close and promising her that you'll never let the world break her, even when it's breaking you. And maybe that's enough. For now, that had to be enough.

Before you cross the street, take my hand. Life is what happens while you're making other plans. - John Lennon

Head Start Program - The Big Red Church Door

In the meantime, I was readmitted to Temple as a junior, and I still desperately needed day care. I later enrolled Saida in a Get Set Program for preschoolers, which worked pretty well, despite the challenging circumstances it presented. The pre-school was located a few short blocks from Temple's campus.

Few people on campus knew that I was a mother. When I told them, most of my peers were delighted and looked at me with admiration and bewilderment. I was the only student they knew who had 2 kids, a house, and a mortgage. I must have looked very strange. They would be wide-eyed, asking me how I had a child. I gave them the short version.

I didn't want to be looked at or treated differently, just because I was a mother. Besides, back then, single women with children rarely went to college, so I was somewhat of an oddball. I certainly didn't want to be 'judged' or treated differently, due to bias, ignorance, or curiosity, so I kept my mommy status close to my chest.

On more than one occasion, I had to bring Sean along with me for a midterm or final. I would borrow a chair from the classroom and have him wait outside my class with crayons and coloring books.

He was a delightful, obedient child, and I never hesitated to reward him afterwards. In the meantime, I grew into a strong, capable, proud mom. Sean must have been about 7 or 8 years old at the time. He was the apple of my eye. I really enjoyed being a mom, even though I didn't really look the part. I looked like any other co-ed, except I was a mother, breaking down walls to make a way forward for my beloved family.

Sean had entered grade school and was doing quite well. He was a "latchkey child" and often came home to an empty house daily while I attended school. I would get home with Saida as quickly as I could. I would call home every afternoon at 3:00 to make sure he was safe at home.

Of course, I made it a point to be home before dark. I taught my little daughter that we both had to go to school every day. So, every morning, I would wake her up with "It's time for you and mommy to get ready for school, let's go!" I turned this morning ritual into a little game. I made a point of dressing us alike, often wearing the same colors or identical outfits, each carrying our own book bag.

It really helped to cement our bond and made us both feel important. We would check each other out in the full-length mirror before we left for the day. We would often wear matching tams, hats, overcoats, and blue jeans with the same color shirts.

I wanted her to feel like she was taking part in what mommy was doing. It helped her to understand what was going on.

My daughter was now potty-trained and could speak very well. The problem was that she was disruptive in class, did not follow instructions, and cried a lot. Get Set Day Care was a federal child-care program that was designed to prepare children for entry into 1st grade.

Saida was just past 2 years old and barely qualified for the program, but I enrolled her anyway. The good thing about Get Set Daycare was that it was located just outside the campus at Temple, and it was free.

I remember one morning we were all decked out and ready to go. I left Saida sitting in the rocking chair downstairs with her hair products next to her on the coffee table. When I came back downstairs, Saida had put hair oil all over herself, her clothes, and the overstuffed rocking chair. She was a mess, and so was I. I slid down to the floor and cried like a baby. I undressed her, washed the gook out of her freshly braided hair, and settled in for the day. By then, it was too late to go to class, so we stayed home and cooked chicken and dumplings. The day was not a total loss.

I used every opportunity to settle in and spend time with my little "monkey", her nickname. When I returned to class, I asked another student if I could Xerox her notes, so I could keep up with the class I'd missed. They knew I rarely missed class and were eager to help me. My peers were very kind and never hesitated to render help whenever I asked them. Yes, a few of them knew I was a mother and went to great lengths to help me. I was a novelty for sure. Today, I remain grateful for their kindness and support. It made a big difference.

The school at the 'big red door' was a large church basement converted into a warm, inviting classroom. Saida liked the school, and I was determined to keep her there. However, her teachers decided that Saida did not fit into the classroom setting and insisted that she be tested for ADD, which was a fairly new concept at the time. Some pediatricians were prescribing Ritalin for these young children, which I was dead set against.

They tried to remove her from the program, which, according to the regulations, was not allowed without just cause. So I fought against her removal from the program and won. It was all I had.

Yes, I knew something was terribly wrong with my baby, especially when I remembered the considerable trauma she must have endured while still in the womb. She came here hurt, damaged, and distressed. I was still struggling with the shock of losing my mother. Unfortunately, I had little to offer by way of emotional support for my little girl at the time.

I carried around a lot of worry and guilt. It hurt to see her struggle with so much adversity stacked against her so young. It broke my already broken heart. I could see and feel that she needed extra help. I endeavored to get her the help she needed and identify the source of her hyperactivity. I located a pediatric physician who specialized in troubled children.

We designed a Behavioral Modification Program to validate the good things Saida did right and ignore the wrong/bad behavior. I presented the plan to her teachers, and together we devised a color code to monitor her behavior at school every day. Red was bad, green was good, and yellow was cautionary. We would also add new colors and smiley faces with gold stars when she did well, which was only about half the time.

During another pediatric appointment, I asked the doctor to look at other outside influences that may contribute to her hyperactivity and her inability to remain in her seat during class. I had my suspicions and was determined to get to the bottom of this. I wanted my baby not to just get by, but to thrive and be her best self. As her mother, I saw this as my primary responsibility.

Later, Saida and I began this little ritual called "relax and read" time. If I had an early class, I would pick her up, and we would head home, put on our pajamas, grab our favorite snacks, and 'relax and read'. She would have her books, and I would have mine. We would spend many afternoons that way, until Sean came home from grade school or something else distracted us. I will always cherish those times we spent together.

RALPH NADER - CONSUMER REPORTS

I became a huge fan of the environmental movement. Before 'Love Canal' (in upstate New York), there was little attention paid to the environmental impact that toxic pesticides, like DDT, had on our health and had entered our food supply. The EPA was newly formed and placed tight restrictions on what companies could add to their food production. I took Saida and Sean to an allergist and determined that both were allergic to sugar and Red Dye #2, both components in most foods we ate daily.

I became acutely aware that I was inadvertently slowly poisoning my children. I immediately took Saida and the whole family off sugary cereals and food with dyes. My kids felt deprived and secretly indulged themselves with forbidden foods whenever they had a chance. Over the next several months, Saida's episodes of hyperactivity slowly began to decrease, but did not entirely disappear.

Ralph Nader put out a magazine called Consumer Reports. It listed the latest information on pesticides and toxins in food production. His magazine was instrumental in helping consumers avoid toxins and the long list of additives that infiltrate our food supply. His work was instrumental in demonstrating the link between what we eat and how it affects our health. Truly, eye-opening.

He also reported on pending and current legislation that impacted the US food and drug industry. Ralph Nader is an advocate for human health and well-being. His book "Unsafe at Any Speed" underscored the necessity for 55 MPH speed limits and mandatory seat belts. A true pioneer I deeply respect.

I do not believe that you should drug children, rather than help them work through their problems and emotions. I clearly remember my own childhood and strove to be empathetic. Yes, even children have problems. I respect that. After all, we are all human. We have faults; we all need some kind of help to overcome obstacles.

Identify them, challenge them, whatever you do, don't ignore it, face it, and defeat it.

HATE KNOWS THAT LOVE IS THE CURE

*L*osing Mommy - Minerva Pinkney

As around the sun, the earth knows she's revolving and the rose-buds know to bloom in early May. Just as hate knows love's the cure you can rest your mind for sure, that I'll be loving you always. – Stevie Wonder

Mommy was sick. Her stomach was growing large, and she was having lots of pain. I went with her to the doctor's office. I believe my brother, Brook, was with us. Somehow, I don't remember much about the doctor's visit. Just the diagnosis. Mommy was not in the room with us. Mom was diagnosed with ovarian cancer. It would kill her in less than 18 months. To say I was devastated was an understatement.

I knew nothing of life, let alone cancer. She had undergone a radical operation to remove the cancerous mass. After the operation, the doctors said there was little hope for recovery. I didn't really believe them. I couldn't afford to. I had to keep going. Unfortunately, they were right. I had just begun taking classes at Temple and was starting to believe that my life might be turning out all right after all. I dropped out of Temple.

I went straight to the Dean's office, right before midterms, and asked to withdraw from all my classes. I received 4 incompletes and was temporarily suspended from school. My professors agreed to enter a grade of incomplete until I could return and complete the classes.

Looking back, that was another very lucky break. Perhaps I still had a chance to graduate from Temple after all. Soon, I began accompanying mommy to her doctor's appointments. The kids and I would often spend the night in my old bedroom on the weekends. Sean was 7, Saida was 1.

Showering Mommy with my love

Being the well-known pest that I am, I began the annoying habit of sleeping with mommy. I would wait until she was asleep and slip into bed beside her. I liked the way she always smelled of Pond's cold cream; her smell gave me comfort. When she realized I was there, she would pop me and demand that I leave, but I never did. I always cuddled close to her so I could smell her cold cream scent.

I took pleasure in annoying her, which I had done gleefully as a child. I returned to my childhood ways and bugged her endlessly just to get a rise out of her. She would say, Janet, will you please leave me alone! I would answer ok, and immediately begin to follow her and sniff her just to aggravate her in some way. I became her baby again. All I wanted to do was be close to her; she never lost her temper or turned me away.

The chemo treatments were hard on her body. We purchased a wig when her thick, long hair began to fall out. She also lost her eyebrows, and it became my appointed duty to fill in her eyebrows when she went anywhere or had visitors. One day, she called me to say that an old flame was coming to visit and could I come to the hospital just to put her eyebrows on ASAP, which I did. Her vanity amused me. Still trying to keep her looks up, despite her condition. I learned from her that you don't have to look like what you've been through.

I would lose the tenuous hold I had on my life. Jeff reappeared when he heard about my divorce. He pleaded with me to give our family a chance. He embraced my little daughter and proceeded to give her large doses of fatherly love. At times, we were actually happy, until disaster struck, once again.

My mother and Jeff's mother were friends. They shared the same birthday. They supported our union and thought that getting married was a good first step in the right direction. Speaking for myself, I was terrified. At that point, I would have willingly danced with the devil, which, as it turns out, I was. The doctors said her illness was terminal, and they asked us not to reveal this fact to my mother, which my brothers and I agreed to. The objective was to help her fight back, nursing the belief that she would get better. For a while, she did get better. For me, things got progressively worse.

Although I had to drop out of school to take care of my mommy, I continued to leave Saida with the sitter.

I did not tell them that I had dropped out of school, so I could be with my mother during appointments and chemo treatments. My depression became more and more unmanageable as I struggled against time to save my mother's life. If this were a matter of my will, or the veracity of my desperate prayers, and love for her, surely, she would survive! My love for her was boundless, and I did not hesitate to postpone my dreams to be there for her.

As usual, I accompanied her to Hahnemann Hospital on Broad Street for her chemo treatments. Typical of mommy, she made friends with everyone. Proudly introducing me to everyone as her 'only daughter'. I remember once her heart slowed and almost stopped during chemo. The doctor decided to admit her, then and there. My fear exploded. I stood staunchly by, trying not to show the absolute terror that had begun to grow heated deep inside my gut.

Mommy loved the soap operas, so I brought her a small portable television, and she and her chemo buddies would gather in her room daily. We watched Search for Tomorrow while munching on forbidden McDonald's lunch, located just across the street from the hospital. I became aware of the fact that she had adopted the other patients who had no one.

No visitors, no one to help them to the bathroom, or bring them snacks, or put make-up on because they could no longer see. She became the queen of the cancer ward. She had a lot of followers who looked forward to my visits as much as she did.

Although children were not allowed on the floor, I snuck them into the room, to the delight of mommy and her new friends. We had a ball. My dad came, and I heard the nurses giggling as we walked together down the long hall...' looks just like him,' they all said, she even walks like him.... Still tall and handsome in his early 50s, he was always turning heads.

I learned a lot about human behavior during that time. My mother grew in compassion and grace as she fought hard against an unseen enemy that neither she nor I knew anything about.

Relatives who were afraid or just plain damn selfish would call me almost daily for updates.

Aunts and cousins that I had known all my life simply disappeared, or called me constantly to assuage their guilt for whatever reason.

Often asking far too many questions that they could answer themselves, if they had bothered to show the fuck up.

Mom began a round of in and out of the hospital. I will never forget an occasion we had to spend the day at her home together. It was the middle of the week. I had gotten Saida all dressed up, and we showed up early that morning to surprise her.

I will never forget the joyful look on her face as she peeped down from her bedroom window, beaming. She was completely bald by then. Often snatching off her wig with a huge smile. Much to the delight of her grandchildren. I learned a lot from her during that time. Mostly, how to stand up to life when you've been handed a bad deal. I never heard her complain about her circumstances; she had class, and she was so brave. I stood staunchly by her side.

Before she died, my mother called me to her bed and said 'I'm dying, Janet, please don't embarrass me with your antics, I know how you act out." I laughed, saying 'nonsense,' but she made me promise anyway. True to my word, I stood steadfast next to her casket during the entire funeral. Sarah Jane sang the Lord's Prayer in her uniquely beautiful soprano voice. I did not cry. I did not act out.

Mommy died in May 1979. I was only 23 years old. I watched them lower my mother into the ground as silent tears rolled down my face. I would never see her again. As time passed, I got used to the sound of her voice urging me on, giving me advice and directions, leading me on. A phenomenon that took quite a lot of getting used to. Fortunately, I learned to heed that strong voice, as she began to guide me through the hell that had become my life.

While I stayed at my mother's house making funeral arrangements, my house was robbed. I was too shocked to react. I filed a police report. Neighbors said they saw Joi and her boyfriend, Greg, enter my house. They denied it, but deep down I knew it was true. I was a sitting duck, and they took mad advantage of my vulnerability. I heard that Greg had gotten Joi hooked on drugs. So much for friendship and love.

Once again, God smiled down on me in my despair. I told my social worker that my house had been robbed, and my beloved IBM typewriter was stolen.

He lent me his own personal typewriter and carefully delivered it to me. I had to petition my school to readmit me, given that I had withdrawn in the middle of my first term at Temple. I needed the typewriter to complete the coursework, critical to meeting my academic requirements, which I did.

TIMING IS EVERYTHING

W hat is the 411 - GRADUATION!

In my mind, I'm going to Carolina,... carry on without me, say nice things about me, 'cause I'm gone. – James Taylor

Tommy Jones

Later that summer, shortly after my mother's death, I went to visit my brother Robert, who had just built a house 'from the ground up' in North Carolina. He and his wife Sheila had been married 10 years before their daughter Sheilita was born. These folks got it right, whether by accident or on purpose; they were on their way.

North Carolina sang to me like a lover that summer, its tall pines and winding roads promising the kind of peace I'd forgotten existed. My brother Robert had built his house there from the dirt up. He and Sheila, waiting ten years before having Sheilita—they'd done it right, planned or luck. James Taylor's words became my prayer.

Enter Thomas Jones, working with my brother Robert at the plant. Dark skin and knowing eyes, treating me like I was worth something. We burned up those Carolina roads with Michael Henderson and Luther Vandross turning the speakers loud.

No Catholic guilt, no five-minute missionary position followed by shame. Just pure pleasure and laughter, something I'd forgotten could exist between a man and woman.

He had two boys, was separated from his wife, and loved me with a heat that made Jeff's tepid touch feel like handcuffs I'd finally slipped. I went to North Carolina and fell in love with life. The timing could not have been better, such a wonderful, peaceful place.

Yes, of course, I was vulnerable and needed a break, just what the doctor ordered. But timing's a bitch, and pressure back home mounted to "do right" by Jeff and the family. Our parents had arranged the marriage before Mommy died, thinking they were saving us both. Like a fool walking into quicksand, I chose the path everyone else wanted.

I promised to leave my Carolina lover alone, sacrificing my happiness for what others thought was best. That's when the real nightmare began.

I wish I knew what it felt like to be free – Nina Simone

When I returned home, I told Jeff about 'the affair' and decided NOT to marry him. My relationship continued openly and unashamedly. I certainly needed more than what 'mama's boy' had to offer. No catholic schoolboy hangups. None of that 5-minute slam bam, thank you ma'am sex, Catholic Church tyranny.

Not to mention Tommy Jones's sex was out of sight. Tommy was very refreshing, light-hearted, and plain fun. I came to realize that I loved being in the country.

The tall NC pines and the wide open, uncluttered roads had really captured my heart. I felt free in a way that I had never felt before. I felt what was missing in my life. I began to imagine my life differently. No nasty subways, no break-ins, no nasty can't fuck, broke ass niggers.

Yes, I could get used to this. The problem was that I was entering my senior year at Temple University and on very thin ice, financially, academically, and emotionally.

I had two small children, a heavy mortgage, school debt, and no help, not to mention that the rug had been pulled from under me due to my mother's untimely death. Yes, I was scared to face life without her. Yes, our parents had arranged our marriage before my Mom died. What did I do? What any smart woman would do. I married Jeff in a panic, my worst enemy, instead of following my heart.

I was aware that quitting school before graduation was suicide. I did not want to abandon my house and leave my degree on the table during my senior year, so I resolved to tough it out and weigh my options once I graduated.

That's when the real fun began. I promised to leave my NC lover alone, in favor of solidifying the family, for the good of all concerned. Who I was or what I wanted never entered the picture. So I married my life's worst enemy. Straight from the frying pan into the fire.

By then, Jeff truly hated me. I had an open affair, was unrepentant, and refused to marry him.

Everyone knew it. Needless to say, we argued frequently; I almost lost my right middle finger during a drunken argument. It was slammed in the door as I tried to leave my own house, running to safety.

During the fight, he confidently yelled that no one could help me. "Your Mother is dead, she can't help you," he shouted proudly! I had to go to the emergency that night. Later, when my regular doctor saw me, he did not recognize me; I had been beaten so badly.

Suddenly, feeling secure didn't matter, but being free did! It was now or never. It became my single-minded goal, not only to get the hell away from Jeff, but to get my kids out of Philadelphia, as soon as possible. I vowed to get my degree and leave town.

Start my life over, just like in the movies. At least that's what I thought, and that's what I set out to do. I was 24 years old. By the time I graduated, it was too late for Tommy and me.

Graduation

It took me a little over 5 years before I graduated. I had taken time off to help my mother. I had taken 2 semesters off to have baby Saida (and get divorced). Some people (family/friends?) made nasty jokes about me, calling me a professional student. I ignored them and kept going.

My children were the reason I never gave up. Plus, I had promised mommy that I would get an education. I aimed to make her proud.

We should keep in mind that before you take on any venture, you must first believe in it yourself. People say, fake it until you make it, but that is only partly true. You must first become that scientist, mathematician, or lawyer, inside, before it can manifest outside.

As much as it's said, it's worth repeating: You must believe in yourself. It was under these circumstances that I grew stronger as a college student and a mother.

My road was rougher because I had so much "skin in the game" or too much to lose if I failed. As time passed, I became more adept at time management and multitasking, even before there were words for it. I began to see myself among many young women who were charting new pathways for our daughters and ourselves.

Street fighters, hell raisers, rebels, yes if you will. It was a heady, exciting time to be a young woman in a thriving city like Philadelphia. I felt empowered by that. In fact, I reveled in it.

The women's movement had a strong effect on me as it did on most women of my generation. We believed strongly that we could have it all: an education, a good salary, a good marriage, and raise great kids. One is not limited by biology or what we are as 'women' could offer ourselves and to the world.

We then set about to prove it, becoming great doctors, lawyers, astronauts, policemen, you name it, we made it happen. Yes, even policemen. Before the women's movement, women were not allowed in the police force or in combat zones.

While I will admit there are some areas that we were a little overly optimistic about, we forged ahead anyway, determined to succeed. Stating emphatically that nothing could stop us from "having it all", which for the most part we did.

I am still so very proud of the inroads we made during that turbulent time.

SAY IT AGAIN FOR THE PEOPLE IN THE BACK

So if you got a lover and you want her for your wife, you got to love her, and love her all her life - (All the way around and back) - Marvin Gaye

Kenneth F. White — Age 54

Unfortunately, I was more attracted to potential rather than reality. I fell for dreams instead of actions. On the subway, on the way to work at Temple University Press one day, I met the man who helped to change my life and to fulfill my dreams of escaping Philadelphia.

His name was Kenneth White; he followed me off the subway and pestered me until he got my telephone number. Kenny was strikingly handsome, having done print ads for a few local department stores.

He had attended Villanova and had taken a few acting classes. In him, I learned to appreciate how show business worked behind the scenes, with supporting actors, walk-ons, character actors, and the like. He also had a few plays under his belt. We both loved the theater.

During high school, I was in a group that often got hold of theater tickets. I told him about seeing James Earl Jones and Jane Alexander in the Great White Hope, and how he brought the audience to their feet with his powerful voice. They later reprised their roles in a film with the same name.

You could feel his emotion. "Here I am, here I am, here I am," he shouted while pounding his massive chest. He gave me shivers. Powerful performance. That, my dear, is true art.

Kenny came from a large 2-parent household. Kenny had a 3-year-old son (Seitu) from a previous relationship. He knew how to put on a decent shirt and tie and had impeccable manners. He loved the nightlife and later took me to Jazz clubs, South Philly, and other hot night spots around town.

We became good phone buddies. We talked almost every night. I found out that we had a lot in common. As a matter of fact, his older brother Lonnie had dated Sarah Jane.

Looking back, I guess you could call it a trauma bond, because I was indeed facing a brand new trauma. The Philadelphia Gas Company had just sent me a bill for $5,000 and turned off the gas. How, you say, is still a mystery. In a panic, I had a friend of mine turn the gas back on illegally.

I had two small kids with asthma, and I was determined to protect them and keep them warm. My other best friend, Felicia, Saida's

Godmother, now living in Georgia, and Jeff were the only other people who knew the gas was on illegally.

Somehow, 'someone' had tipped them off that the gas was turned back on. Even though I was playing it safe, I had a space heater, and we all slept together. I made dinner on trays (this was before microwaves), and made a game out of eating dinner in front of the kerosene heater. The ground outside was frozen solid, and we were cold, but we were safe, we were warm, and we were together.

I called in sick from work the very next day, and promptly got fired. I guess I was too ashamed to show up to work with the black eye that Jeff had given me days before. Forget about domestic violence; it wasn't discussed, unless you were on the Phil Donahue Show or something.

Talk about brainstorming, I put together a fake lease and had an old high school friend stand in as the new tenant. Not surprisingly, the same fiend from the Gas Company came back to make sure it wasn't me, but it was. I was upstairs listening, praying. God was with me; he bought the ruse and we had heat. Things were turning around, finally.

Kenny came to my house and saw how Jeff had torn it up while I was at work. Kicking in doors, knocking holes in walls, cutting up the kids' baby pictures, destroying my grandmother's clothes, and precious heirlooms. I had recently lost my beloved Mom-Mom a few months earlier. He even sprayed graffiti on the walls and cut up my mattress.

Obviously, Jeff didn't care how this would affect his children; of course, they were terrified. Kenny felt sorry for me and decided to stay at my house for a few nights to watch over us. We were not lovers then. Later, we did the best we could to repair the house. Together, Kenny, me, and my youngest brother Eric (who had recently moved in after his stint in the Army), fixed up the house to prepare it for a new tenant. It took over 18 months.

Another Miracle

Once again, the angels smiled down on me. On a routine visit to the local unemployment office, unbeknownst to me, my application was submitted to a local TV community service program called "Project Working". It seemed that as a recent college graduate, I had a pretty good chance at snagging a job.

I became the subject of a local news cast, which followed people who were looking for a job. The local network (WCAU, Channel 10) sent a camera crew to my house and interviewed me about my job search and career path. The person who interviewed me hinted that she had a surprise for me, but didn't tell me what it was. A clip from the interview was used as an advertisement for the program. The promo ran once per hour for about a month.

I remember waking up to the sound of my own voice; to say I was surprised was an understatement. I went from broke and unemployed to hometown celebrity overnight. Job offers were coming out of the woodwork. I had my pick, which was unbelievable considering all I had been through. I was finally able to obtain gainful employment and pay my bills, like a normal human being.

I became involved in local politics, volunteering for the election of the first black mayor of Philadelphia W. Wilson Goode. Kenny and I attended the victory party. It was elevating, life-affirming. The city had suffered for years under the tyranny of Frank Rizzo and his goons.

My brothers were constantly harassed by the police, who were openly hostile and violent towards their black citizens, especially the Black Panthers, and any and all black people, forced to live in a hostile, segregated society. I held fast to my dream of leaving Philadelphia; now I was leaving it in good hands

Kenny and I got buddy passes to visit my old friend (Saida's Godmother), Felicia (Aunt Lee), in Atlanta. He wanted to get the hell out of Philadelphia too. I loved Atlanta for all the obvious reasons: fresh air and sunshine, birthplace of freedom movement, home of Spelman and Morehouse Colleges.

I was all in. I just hadn't quite figured out exactly how I was going to pull this off. I had never lived anywhere else; Philadelphia was all I knew. I guess that's precisely why I needed to leave. I was still grieving for my mother when I got the news that my father was very ill. This was only 3 years after my mother passed. I put on my Superman cape and flew into action, again.

MY DADDY

Willie *Pinkney, Sr. - Age 56*

Lonely Teardrops... my pillow is never dry – Jackie Wilson

I put together a fine Sunday dinner. I'm not sure if I remember who was there; I'm sure my brothers, Brook & Eric, were there. We had a great time. Little did I know it would be our last meal with our dad. A few weeks later, my dad was admitted to the VA hospital, where we determined that his condition was terminal. Nothing happened overnight.

Jeff and I had officially separated months earlier. Jeff had broken into my house and tried to beat me up in front of my kids, again. He had heard that I was seeing someone (which was not true at the time), and the divorce was not yet final. I guess he felt he had a right to my person and my possessions. I called in sick from work the very next day, and promptly got fired. I guess I was too ashamed to show up to work with a black eye. Forget about domestic violence; it wasn't discussed, unless you were on the Phil Donahue Show or something.

One night, I got the dreaded call. My father had taken a turn for the worse; there was no time to gather the other siblings. Eric, Kenny, and I jumped in the car and rushed to the hospital. No cell phones: we were told that we had to make a decision right then and there, no waiting for the rest of the family. Eric and I were the only ones there; we were out of time. My dad was on a ventilator, and I watched helplessly as his chest rose and fell forcefully, and against his rather considerable will. He continued to breathe.

Here was a man of great talent and fortitude, dying too young from alcoholism. I knew that he would not approve of being kept alive against his will. So, I decided to turn off his life support; I knew he was already gone. I held his hand while Eric and I watched his vital signs fade. I had to fight the urge to straddle him and choke him for breaking my heart. I remember thinking, 'How could you do this to us, how?'. Yes, I was sad at the loss, but what was more disturbing was that his death could have been prevented. He died of liver disease, after years of drinking, dire warnings, and a lifetime of pain.

The funeral taught me everything I needed to know about staging a burial in hostile territory. Curly is fighting us every step, the family taking sides, me catching hell from all directions while trying to give my father a decent burial. My house slipped into foreclosure status, but I couldn't let him go into a pauper's grave. Not my daddy. Not the man who still turned heads at fifty-something, who gave me his good looks, his walk, and his pride. Yes, I am a shameless spoiled daddy's girl. Despite his shortcomings, I always knew that he loved me. He never turned his back on me. I loved him with all my heart.

Now my brothers and I had to plan a funeral. That's when we discovered that he did not have life insurance. His longtime girlfriend, Curly, had a small policy, but refused to release it because she didn't want my father to be buried next to my mother. After all, my parents were still married. My brothers and I wanted them to be buried next to each other. At one point, they really did love each other.

After all was said and done, I wanted to honor that. Given that Curly refused to cooperate, my family was faced with having to raise about $10,000.00 in less than 7 days. Which we did. It took extraordinary effort, and I got a crash course in staging and paying for a funeral in a hostile, aggravating environment. All while catching hell. I even put in two mortgage payments, which, of course, placed my house in jeopardy and in foreclosure status.

Earlier, I sent Saida down to Atlanta with her Godmother Felicia (Aunt Lee) as I got busy preparing to leave Philadelphia for good. The move was delayed because of the deaths of my father and Grandmother within the previous 14 months. I didn't really have time to grieve. I had no choice but to just keep pushing on, which I did.

When I finally hit Atlanta, Saida was there waiting for me. Six years old, soft eyes, my world wrapped in tiny fingers. She'd been away for months, under Aunt Lee's care, and my gratitude was deep, but life had a way of laughing at your best plans. Felicia, the same Felicia who was supposed to have my back, had bought a house with two damn mortgages and ended up in foreclosure. And just to twist the knife, my own house was in foreclosure, too. I had used that mortgage money to help bury my father. Family first, but it came at a price. I was trying to catch up, but it was like running in wet sand.

When Felicia dropped her own bomb that her house was facing foreclosure, too, there was a shift in the atmosphere. Although I had been sending money to her while Saida was living there, it was not enough. She'd joined some Islamic sect that allowed multiple wives but didn't enforce support, leaving women and children in poverty while men moved on to fresh beds. We fought ugly, painful fights, turning friends into enemies.

Kenny had arrived in Atlanta by then. She kicked us all out. My baby girl was very close to her Aunt Lee. She had an asthma attack, taking her breath just as Atlanta took mine. That's how I learned where the East Point hospital was running my child to the emergency ward in a strange city where I didn't know shit about anything.

Kenny and I were always getting lost. Felicia had done the best she could, but failed to inform me of how bad her situation was. I was still in the process of catching up on the mortgage on my Philly house. I put my house on the rental market and had a real estate friend of mine give me the security deposit in order to move to Atlanta. I prayed, real hard...

Fortunately, I had the foresight to have my income tax return check mailed to my brother Brook's house (this was way before direct deposit). He would step in many times to help me along this journey. My resume was sharp and ready to go. My college degree was newly minted.

The plan was to get hired by a bank and obtain a mortgage, buy that dream house in the country... live with my new partner, Kenny... create a safe haven for my children and my brothers, become a strong, prosperous family, much like the Cosbys, remember? We were all still reeling from the deaths of our mother, father, and grandmother. Personally, I thought it was time to get rid of some of the heartbreak and loss we all had suffered and start a new life in beautiful sunny Atlanta. But wait, not so fast.

THE SAGA OF PALMETTO

Finding Palmetto

Phyllis Thompson – Age 73

The airport was expanding in College Park, a small town next to East Point. Many homeowners were being displaced, and just left their homes vacant. Some of these properties came on the market through a popular concept in the south called house moving—taking homes off their foundations and placing them on new land, creating instant equity if you were lucky.

That's where I met Phyllis Thompson at the MARTA bus stop on a muggy Tuesday morning in June. She was waiting for the same bus I took to work downtown, a stylish woman in her late sixties with silver hair swept into a neat bun and the kind of posture that spoke of better days. When she heard my Philadelphia accent, her face lit up.

"Pittsburgh," she said, extending her hand. We struck up one of those easy conversations that happen between women who've both traveled far from home. Phyllis worked as a seamstress, taking in alterations for soldiers at Fort McPherson. I worked for the bank, also located on base. Phyllis lived in Club Candlewood too, in East Point, but had her sights set on something bigger.

"I found some land out in Palmetto," she told me that first morning, her eyes bright with possibility. "Two and a half acres for next to nothing. Going to move a house out there, have my own little piece of America." Palmetto. I'd never heard of it, but the way she said it made it sound like the Promised Land.

Over the next few weeks, Phyllis and I became bus-stop friends, then real friends. She'd show me pictures of the land rolling hills covered in pine trees, red dirt roads that disappeared into green shadows. "You should come see it," Phyllis said one morning. "Bring that handsome man of yours. There's another lot right next to mine."

Kenny and I drove out there on a Saturday in July. The man at the gas station, an elderly Black gentleman (dubbed the man who lived to give directions) who seemed to live in a rocking chair beside the old gas station, pointed us in the right direction with a wide smile.

We'd later learn that this was simply "the old guy who gives directions." No one seemed to know his real name, but he was Palmetto's unofficial welcome committee, a living GPS system who could direct you to anyone's property, tell you who was kin to whom, and provide a running commentary on the town's gossip. He became our landmark, our anchor point in a place where addresses were more suggestion than fact.

Phyllis's land was everything she'd promised. Rolling hills that seemed to go on forever, pine trees that whispered secrets in the Georgia breeze, and silence so complete you could hear your own heartbeat. Kenny and I walked the property line, dreaming out loud about the house we'd build, the garden I'd plant, the peace we'd finally find.

"This is it," I told Phyllis that day. "This is where we start over." We put a small down payment on the lot next to hers and began making plans. Phyllis had already contracted with a house-moving company to relocate a three-bedroom cottage from College Park. Kenny and I found a similar deal, a house that needed to be moved to make way for airport expansion.

For weeks, we'd drive out to Palmetto on Sundays, walking our land, measuring spaces, planning where the driveway would go. Phyllis would pack a picnic lunch and we'd eat under the big oak tree, talking about vegetable gardens and front porch swings, about having space to breathe and room for family to visit.

"I've been dreaming about this since I was a girl," Phyllis told me one afternoon, lying on her back in the tall grass, staring up at the clouds. "My own land. My own house. Nobody can tell me to move along, pay higher rent, make myself smaller."

I understood that feeling. All my life, I'd been at someone else's mercy, absent landlords, mortgages, broken husbands, and too many circumstances far beyond my control. But land was permanent. Land was power. Land was the American Dream in its purest form.

The house moving was scheduled for early September. Phyllis's cottage would go first, then ours the following week. We'd spend the fall getting settled, winterizing the properties, and by spring, we'd be living the dream. But dreams have a way of turning into nightmares when you're Black in rural Georgia.

The trouble started as soon as word got out that we'd bought land on the "white" side of Palmetto. The town was small enough that everyone knew everyone's business, and apparently, some folks weren't happy about the new neighbors.

It began with small things. Our survey stakes disappeared. Our eyes darted nervously toward a group of white men who'd taken to hanging around the store. In 1984, Georgia, that wasn't exactly breaking news.

She'd lived through Jim Crow, raised children during the Civil Rights Movement, buried a husband who'd died fighting for his country, only to come home and be treated like a second-class citizen. "They can call all they want," she told me, her jaw set in determination. "I got the deed to that land. I got my rights."

The morning they moved her house, I took the day off work to be there. It was a sight to behold, this little white cottage loaded onto a massive trailer, creeping down Highway 29 like some kind of architectural parade. Phyllis stood beside me, tears streaming down her face, watching her dream inch closer to reality.

The house movers were professional and efficient. By evening, Phyllis's cottage sat on its new foundation, looking like it had always belonged among the pine trees. She insisted on sleeping there that first night, even though there was no electricity or running water yet. "I want to wake up on my own land," she said.

I received a panicked call from Phyllis. Her house was on fire. I left the bank in the middle of the afternoon and drove those winding roads with my heart in my throat. I could smell the smoke before I could see it. That acrid, bitter smell that meant something precious was burning.

Phyllis's house was gone. Not damaged, not partially burned. Gone. Reduced to a pile of charred timber and twisted metal, smoke still rising from the ruins like incense for broken dreams. Phyllis stood in what had been her front yard, still wearing the house dress she'd slept in, staring at the destruction with dry eyes. The fire department was packing up its equipment.

The sheriff was taking notes on a clipboard, asking questions no one wanted to answer. "Started around three in the morning," one of the firefighters told me. "By the time we got here, there wasn't nothing to save."

I put my arms around Phyllis, expecting her to collapse into sobs, but she stood rigid as a pine tree, her dignity intact even in the face of such cruelty. "They waited until I was asleep," she said quietly. "Cowards always wait until you're asleep."

The sheriff, a thin white man with cold eyes and a mouth like a paper cut, barely looked at us as he delivered his verdict. "Probably electrical," he said, not even trying to sound convincing. "Old house, new wiring. These things happen." But there was no electricity, so that explanation didn't fit.

"These things happen." As if Black dreams spontaneously combust. As if forty-seven years of saving and planning could be erased by faulty wiring that had worked fine for decades before being moved to the "wrong" side of town.

"I'm too old to fight this fight again," she told me when I asked if she wanted to press charges, demand an investigation, make some noise. "Some battles, you got to choose which ones are worth dying for."

I drove Phyllis back to East Point that day, her few salvaged possessions in the back of my Honda. She never talked about rebuilding, never mentioned the land again. Within a month, she'd put the scorched property up for sale and secured another property further south in Hogansville, GA. Where she began renovation on an old farmhouse.

Later, she started her own clothing line, "Styles by Phyllis", which became very successful. She sold her clothing line to local boutiques and small dress shops. Being her own boss was a lifelong dream. I was happy for her.

Our house never made it to Palmetto. When the movers tried to lift it off its foundation, the whole structure collapsed like a house of cards. Rotten timbers, they said. Structural damage they hadn't seen before. Another dream reduced to splinters and dust.

It didn't mention the hard work it took to try, the dignity she maintained in defeat, or the lesson she taught me about choosing your battles with courage and conviction.

But I remember. I remember her standing in that burned-out yard, surrounded by the ashes of her American Dream, refusing to let them see her cry. I remember the way she said "Palmetto" that first morning at the bus stop, like it was made of gold and honey.

But you try anyway. You have to try. Because the alternative, accepting that your place in this world is limited by the color of your skin, the circumstances of your birth, the fear in other people's hearts, is no alternative at all.

I got our deposit back, most of it, and we found a different house in Palmetto, this one already built, already standing. A three-bedroom place on the "right/white" side of the railroad tracks that divided the town like a scar. It wasn't the dream house, but it was safe, clean, and new. It was a shelter. It was a place to start over, even if starting over meant accepting that some dreams come with a price too high to pay.

The house in Palmetto became our home, our refuge, our proof that we could make something good grow even in hostile soil. But I never forgot Phyllis Thompson, never forgot her burned-down house and her raw determination to succeed in spite of the odds.

We lost Phyllis to a stroke many years later. She was a heavy smoker. Her daughter Angie, along with her beautiful grand-daughter, Maleeya (the spitting image of Phyllis) were struggling alone to care for her mother. Whenever she needed help, to run errands, or to go to doctor appointments, I came over to help out. It was the least I could do for one so deserving of support.

By then, she could barely speak, but the look of gratitude and love in her eyes was the only payment I needed. I felt honored to be there for her in her final days. She was a strong, independent woman whom I admired greatly.

Phyllis died several years later after a stroke. Her obituary mentioned her years as a seamstress, her devotion to her church, her clothing label, her love of family and friends, and her open, loving, caring heart. It didn't mention the dream that burned to ashes on a September night in rural Georgia. It didn't need to; this lady stood strong against tyranny and showed no signs of defeat. I was proud of Phyllis, a powerful force, a wonderful friend, who was always there for me and my family, whatever the need.

Brook called our new place "Mayberry," teasing that soon I'd be out in the woods picking berries. He and his wife, Mimi, gave us the down payment for the house and were frequent visitors to our new haven. Despite everything, the threats, the fire, the collapsed dreams, Palmetto felt like home. Or the closest thing to home, after fleeing for my life from Philadelphia.

The dream was still alive, just different than I'd imagined. Not the wide open acres and custom-built house I'd envisioned, but a three-bedroom rental on the right side of the tracks. Not the partnership with Phyllis I'd hoped for, but the memory of her courage when everything fell apart.

Sometimes the dream you get isn't the dream you wanted. But it's yours. And that, I was learning, had to be enough.

Driving 285

Having my tax return mailed to Brook's house was the smartest thing I ever done. My resume was sharp, my degree still fresh, with dreams of my banking job enabling me to obtain a mortgage. Kenny and I wanted to build a solid life, strong, prosperous, unbreakable family. My family was still suffering from losing Mommy, Daddy, and Grandmother so quickly.

Maybe that's exactly what we all needed, a fresh start. I was determined to help my brothers recover from so much loss and gain some much needed assets. Atlanta was richly green and wide open. Land was cheap, undeveloped, and readily available. Atlanta was a great place to start when compared to Philadelphia.

Through it all, Mommy's voice stayed with me, ghostly whispers guiding me. On some nights, I'd hear her clear as day, giving advice, showing me the path forward. It took time to get used to conversations with the dead, but Mommy's wisdom never steered me wrong. She taught me how to walk through fire without turning to ash, how to stand tall when life hands you nothing but broken pieces and expects you to build a castle from rubble.

SHAKE THE DUST OFF

I Choose Freedom

You got a fast car, I want a ticket to anywhere, maybe we can make a deal, maybe together we can get somewhere... – Tracey Chapman

Driving Blind

I did finally get a job at a local bank, after a false start with the first bank I applied to. Banks were heavily regulated at the time, so it was almost unheard of for a bank to go bankrupt. I felt that I had a secure job that I could move up in. However, that was only partly true.

The commute from Palmetto to downtown Atlanta was a beast, over an hour each way on a good day, longer when traffic backed up on I-85 or when our old Honda decided to have one of its temperamental episodes.

But I was grateful for steady work, grateful for the health insurance, grateful for a chance to use my college degree in something that resembled a career.

Kenny would drop me off at the MARTA station in College Park on his good days, when our car was running, and he was feeling motivated. On his bad days, which were becoming more frequent.

The Pattern Emerges

Kenny had arrived in Atlanta with grand plans. He was going to break into the film industry. Atlanta was becoming a major production hub, and with his theater background and good looks, surely, he could find work as an extra or maybe even land a speaking role.

For the first few months, it seemed possible. He got a job with the Atlanta Housing Authority, a decent position with benefits and room for advancement.

I was proud of him, proud of us, proud of the life we were building in our little house in Palmetto.

But Kenny had what I came to recognize as a chronic case of "grass is greener" syndrome. No job was ever quite right, no supervisor appreciated his talents, no workplace understood his creative ambitions.

There was always something wrong with the hours, the commute, the office politics, the lack of artistic fulfillment.

I bit my tongue, remembering all the mornings I'd had to wake him up, all the times our neighbor had to wait while Kenny got dressed, all the complaints about his chronic lateness that he'd brushed off.

Something better. Always something better on the horizon while the bills piled up on our kitchen table, and I worked myself into exhaustion trying to keep us above water.

The Revelation

I should have seen it coming, but denial is a powerful drug. I was so busy working, so busy trying to hold everything together, that I missed the obvious signs. Or maybe I didn't want to see them.

The bank statement arrived on Thursday. I almost didn't open it. Balancing our finances had become an exercise in creative math, moving money from one account to another, robbing Peter to pay Paul. But something made me tear open that envelope, maybe the same instinct that had kept me alive through all the other disasters in my life.

I opened the statement with much trepidation, with shaking hands. There it was, in neat rows of computerized type: his paycheck deposits from the Atlanta Housing Authority, right up until the present day. No wage garnishment. No deductions for child support. Just his full salary, every two weeks, is deposited and then quickly withdrawn.

While I'd been scraping together money for groceries and utilities, while I'd been picking up every freelance gig I could find, while I'd been lying awake at night wondering how we'd make rent, Kenny had been collecting a steady paycheck and spending it on... what? Clothes? Meals out? A new car?

I couldn't tell from the bank statement, but I could see enough to know he'd been lying to me. "Garnishment for child support," he'd said when I asked why he wasn't contributing to household expenses. "They take most of my check before I even see it."

I sat at our kitchen table, staring at those numbers, feeling the familiar burn of betrayal in my chest. How many times was I going to let someone lie to me?

How many times was I going to make excuses for men who treated me like a convenience rather than a partner?

When Kenny came home that evening, from wherever he spent his days now that he wasn't working, I had the bank statement spread out on the table like evidence in a criminal trial. "We need to talk," I said. He saw the papers and had the grace to look uncomfortable, but not guilty. Never guilty. "I can explain," he started.

"Don't." I held up my hand. "Don't insult my intelligence by explaining why you lied to me about money while I worked myself half to death trying to support us

"Opportunities." I laughed, but there was no humor in it. "There are always opportunities with you, Kenny. Always something bigger and better just around the corner while I handle the real world."

"You don't have to handle everything alone."

"Yes, I do. Because every time I count on you to handle something, you either quit, walk away, or lie about it."

We sat in silence for a moment, the weight of too many disappointments pressing down between us. Kenny wasn't a bad man; he'd never hit me, never cheated on me, never said a cruel word to my children. But he was a child playing dress-up in a grown man's clothes, and I was tired of being his mother.

"Pack your things," I said finally.

I already found you an apartment in East Point. I filled out the application, paid the deposit, and even gave them my name as a reference. All you have to do is show up."

He stared at me as if I'd spoken in a foreign language. "You can't be serious."

"I divided everything fifty-fifty. Sheets, towels, dishes, furniture. I even got you your own phone line so you can call Philadelphia without running up my bill."

"This is our home."

"This is my home, Kenny. You've been a guest here, and now it's time to go."

Learning to Say No

Moving Kenny out was harder emotionally than practically. We'd been together for several years, and despite his flaws, he'd been there during some of my darkest moments.

He'd held me when I cried about my father's death, helped me paint the walls of our Philadelphia house, and made me laugh during long evenings when the future seemed uncertain.

But love wasn't enough. It never was. Love couldn't pay bills or provide stability or build the kind of partnership I needed to raise my children and create a real home.

Later, after Kenny left, I sat in our suddenly too-quiet house and made a list not of groceries or bills, but of the patterns I kept repeating.

Jeff, who'd been charming and attentive until he wasn't. Billy, who'd promised me a future but couldn't hold a job long enough to make it a reality.

Now Kenny, who'd swept me off my feet with his good looks and theater stories, couldn't sustain the basic responsibility of adult life. By then, we had been together for several years, and our families were close, but I still had to accept the fact that things would not work out for us, no matter how hard I tried. The fact is, I could not have made it in Atlanta without his loving kindness and generosity.

Looking back, I am deeply grateful for his love and devotion. We remained close friends for the rest of his life. Honestly, Kenny was a wonderful, generous man.

Without his help, we probably would not have made it in Atlanta. I will always be grateful for his presence in my life. I will always love and honor him.

Unfortunately, I was more attracted to potential rather than reality. I fell for dreams instead of actions. I kept trying to save people who didn't or couldn't be saved, and in the process, I was drowning.

Finding My Footing

With Kenny gone, I finally had to learn to drive like my life depended on it, because it did. The commute to the bank became my responsibility alone, no more catching rides or depending on someone else's schedule.

I'd gotten my license just before Kenny left, barely passing the test when our old Honda kept stalling on the hill outside the DMV. The examiner, probably tired of dealing with nervous drivers and unreliable cars, passed me just to get me out of her hair.

The crowd of other test-takers who'd been waiting behind us broke into applause when I finally managed to parallel park without hitting anything.

Now I was on my own, navigating Atlanta's highways with the confidence of someone who'd learned to drive out of necessity rather than choice. I-285 became my daily nemesis, a concrete river of aggressive drivers and construction delays. But I learned to hold my own, to merge with authority, to find alternate routes when traffic backed up.

The car troubles continued, with transmission problems, brake issues, and the occasional mysterious noise that meant expensive trips to the mechanic. But they were my problems now, my decisions, my solutions.

When the Honda finally died completely in the parking lot of a Kroger, I didn't call Kenny or any other man to rescue me. I called a tow truck, took it to a mechanic I'd researched, and used money from my small emergency fund to get it fixed.

Financial independence felt different from what I'd expected. Scarier in some ways, every decision was mine, every mistake had consequences only I would face. But there was freedom in it too. I could buy what I needed without justifying it to someone else. I could plan for my children's future without worrying about a partner's unreliable contributions. I could come home to my own space, arranged the way I liked it, peaceful and predictable.

The evenings were the hardest. The house would settle into a quiet that sometimes felt lonely rather than peaceful. But I learned to fill those hours with things that mattered: reading books I'd been too tired to enjoy, taking long baths without someone asking what I was doing in there for so long, sitting on my front porch and listening to the Georgia night sounds without having to make conversation.

For the first time in my adult life, I wasn't waiting for someone else to save me, fix me, complete me, or disappoint me. I was simply being myself, figuring out who that was when I wasn't trying to accommodate someone else's limitations. The driving got easier. The loneliness faded. The bills got paid.

And slowly, quietly, I started to realize that maybe I'd been looking for security in all the wrong places.

Maybe home wasn't something you built with another person; maybe it was something you created for yourself, something no one could take away, something that started with knowing your own worth and refusing to settle for less.

The old Honda kept running, held together by prayer and regular maintenance. I learned to check the oil, replace windshield wipers, and negotiate with mechanics. I learned the routes that avoided the worst traffic, the gas stations with the cleanest bathrooms, and the drive-through that served decent coffee at reasonable prices.

I learned to drive my own life, finally, after years of being a passenger in other people's plans. And that, more than any relationship, felt like freedom.

SETTING BOUNDARIES

We Got Nowhere Else To Go

The phone call came on a Thursday morning while I was getting ready for work at the bank. Debby Nelson's voice cracked through the receiver, desperation bleeding through her words like watercolor on wet paper.

"Janet, I need help. We got nowhere else to go."

I'd known Debby since we were kids in Philadelphia, one of those friendships forged in the projects where you learned early that sometimes all you had was each other. She'd been living in an abandoned house in the Frankfort section of Philly with her two boys, Devon and Damon, ages eight and ten.

Her parents had finally said enough was enough and threatened to call social services if she didn't get her act together.

"I saved up my income tax refund," she said. "I can get down there. I just need a place to land while I figure things out."

Saida was getting ready for school, and the morning routine felt so normal, so stable. The house in Palmetto had become our refuge, three bedrooms, a big backyard where Sean could run, the kind of quiet that only came when you put distance between yourself and the chaos of city life.

But Debby's voice carried that familiar desperation, the same tone I'd heard from too many women who'd been beaten down by circumstances and men who disappeared when things got tough. The same tone I'd used myself more times than I cared to remember.

"You can come," I heard myself saying, "but just temporarily". And Debby, you can't bring the boys until you have your own place. I don't have room for three extra people, and my house needs to stay peaceful for my kids." There was a pause. Then: "I understand. I'll figure something out for them," she said.

Three weeks later, Kenny drove to Philadelphia in a rented U-Haul and brought Debby back. When that truck pulled into my driveway, my heart sank. Instead of a few suitcases and maybe a television, Debby had loaded up an entire household's worth of furniture sofas, dining room sets, bedroom furniture, boxes upon boxes of belongings.

I walked out to the truck, trying to keep my voice level. "Debby, where exactly did you think you were going to put all this?"

She looked at me with those same pleading eyes from childhood, the ones that had gotten us both in trouble more times than I could count. "I thought maybe the garage, or the basement. I used the whole tax refund to buy this stuff. I couldn't leave it behind."

I warned her NOT to do that because she would need a car. She bought furniture instead. I was furious!

"This isn't Philly, Debby. This is rural Georgia. The bus comes once a day and stops at the highway. You'll have to walk everywhere down here." The bus stop was over a mile away.

But the truck was already half-empty, my garage filling up with someone else's life decisions. I felt that familiar weight settling on my shoulders, the weight of other people's problems becoming mine to solve.

I helped her get a job at the local hospital, low wages but steady. The "Mighty 180" bus line had a stop about a mile from the house, so every morning at 5:30, I'd drive Debby to the bus stop and every evening at 6, I'd drive back to pick her up. It wasn't the arrangement I'd signed up for, but it was temporary.

Everything was always temporary.

Within two months, Debby's parents called. They couldn't keep Devon and Damon anymore. The boys were acting out in school, asking when their mother was coming back, and her father's patience had run thin.

"Just bring them," Debby begged when she got off the phone. "Just for a few weeks until I get on my feet."

I looked at my own kids. Sean was twelve, going through his awkward phase, and Saida was still adjusting to the move from East Point. The last thing they needed was more disruption.

"One month," I said finally. "One month, and then you need to have your own place."

The boys arrived, looking lost and scared. Damon, the older one, looked just like Debby's father who was a hard-working man who provided well for his family.

Devon was smaller, quieter, the kind of kid who observed every-thing and said little. They'd been bounced around so much they knew how to make themselves invisible.

I set up sleeping bags in the living room and laid down the rules: homework first, no fighting, help with chores, and respect for everyone in the house. For the first week, they were model chil-dren, grateful, polite, eager to please.

Debby meets Neighborhood Young Lover

He was barely out of high school, working part-time at a local store. All swagger and smooth talk, the kind of boy who could make a lonely woman forget she had responsibilities. Debby started coming home late, her hospital uniforms wrinkled, that glow in her cheeks that had nothing to do with the Georgia sun.

Debby had recently moved into her own apartment nearby, largely because I insisted that she keep her promise to get her own apartment, ASAP. Her son Devon started bringing his little brother to my kitchen table every evening, both of them looking hungry and tired.

I'd make them dinner, pack their school lunches, and try not to show how angry I was becoming.

"She locked us out," Damon told me one afternoon while Devon was in the bathroom. "When he comes over, she tells us to go play outside and not come back till dark."

My hands shook as I helped him with his homework. This sweet, quiet boy shouldn't have to whisper about being locked out of his own home. Shouldn't have to worry about where his next meal was coming from or whether his mother cared enough to make sure he had clean clothes for school. Debby did not own a washer or dryer, so laundry was done at my house.

I started buying extra food in my house, doing their laundry along with my own, helping with homework, and school projects. Debby was actually a very good cook. In fact, she hosted plenty of parties and fun gatherings at her place.

Unfortunately, she was inconsistent when it came to caring for her own children. Sean, bless his heart, took his cousins under his wing, teaching them to play basketball and sharing his video games. Saida complained about the crowding but never said it in front of the boys.

Debby's children, who had been bounced around like ping-pong balls, finally felt safe somewhere, even if it wasn't with their own mother. I wished her the best and hoped that she would take her responsibilities seriously.

Years later, I would think about those months and realize they taught me something crucial about the difference between helping and enabling. I'd spent so much of my life taking care of other people's problems that I'd forgotten when compassion ended and co-dependence began.

But I learned to say no. Learned that sometimes the kindest thing you can do for someone is let them face the consequences of their choices. Learning that you can't save people who don't want to be saved, you can only protect the innocent ones caught in the crossfire.

The house felt quiet after they left, too quiet sometimes. But it was my quiet. My peace. And for the first time in a long time, that felt like enough.

IT IS HARD BUT NECESSARY

S ave Yourself First

My brother, Willie Pinkney Jr., dubbed "June", though nobody called him that, had been my closest sibling growing up. We'd shared clothes, friends, adventures, and that special bond that comes from being the middle children in a family of 6 kids.

"Jersey. Got discharged from the Army last month." A pause, then quieter: "Things got complicated."

Complicated. In June's vocabulary, that could mean anything from a bar fight to something much worse. He'd been stationed at Fort Dix, doing well as far as I knew, but the Army had been his refuge from a world that hadn't made sense since our mother died. Without that structure, that purpose, my older twin brother was adrift.

"Can I come stay with you for a while? Just until I get back on my feet. I got nowhere else to go." June said.

"Of course you can come," I heard myself saying, even as my newly independent self whispered warnings I wasn't ready to hear.

June's Arrival

When I saw my brother, he didn't look the same. Always in motion. This man was thin, jumpy, his eyes darting around the bus station like he expected trouble to find him at any moment.

But when he saw me, his face lit up with that familiar smile, and for a moment, he was my twin brother again.

"Look at you," he said, hugging me tight. "All grown up and living in Georgia like some kind of Southern belle."

I laughed and hugged him back, breathing in the familiar scent of him. Old Spice aftershave and something else, something medicinal I couldn't place. "Look at you, Mr. Army Man. You're skinnier than a fence post."

"Army food," he said, but his laugh didn't reach his eyes.

I wanted to ask more, but something in his posture warned me off. Whatever had happened in New Jersey, whatever had brought him to my doorstep with nothing but a duffel bag and desperation, he wasn't ready to talk about it.

He slept on my couch. Sean was twelve then, old enough to be excited about having his uncle around. Saida, nine and more observant than her years, watched June with curious eyes.

I knew that feeling intimately and had lived with it for years during my marriages, during my mother's illness, during all the times

I'd felt trapped by circumstances beyond my control. But something in June's voice suggested he was drowning in waters much deeper than anything I'd experienced.

June had his own transportation, the 'Thunder Chicken," a used Thunderbird, that he kept looking sharp. He quickly got a job at the now-defunct Eastern Airlines, and as far as I knew, he was on his way up.

What was not known was that he had been dating a woman named Adrienne, and together they began to use crack cocaine, it was the new drug of choice in the 80's. The choice to use crack started the slow descent that would become his life for the next 20 years.

The Downward Spiral

The first time I found the pipe, I didn't know what it was. A small glass tube was hidden in the back of his dresser drawer, pushed behind his socks when I was putting away laundry. I held it up to the light, puzzled, then put it back where I'd found it. I confronted June about the pipe and the strange smells coming from my basement, not wanting to believe what part of me already knew.

The signs were all there if I'd been willing to see them. The weight loss continued even though I cooked good meals every night. The jittery energy was followed by crashes that left him sleeping for fourteen hours straight.

The way he'd disappear for hours and come back with stories that didn't quite add up, errands that took too long, friends I'd never heard of, places that seemed to shift in his telling.

The gas lighting was subtle but effective. Maybe I was working too much. Maybe I was losing track of things. Maybe I was being paranoid, suspicious, unfair to my brother, who was going through a rough time and needed my support.

The Stranger in My House

But then I started paying attention. Living with someone in active addiction is like living with a shapeshifter. One day you're talking to your brother, the person you've known all your life, and the next day you're facing a stranger who looks like him but acts like someone else entirely.

The June I knew was gentle, funny, and protective of family. This new June was paranoid, aggressive, and impossible to predict. He'd be sweet with the kids one moment and snapping at them the next. He'd promise to help with household chores and then disappear. He'd swear he was clean, that he was getting help, that things would be different. Sean, who'd been so excited to have his uncle living with us, began asking when June was going to leave.

"Is Uncle June sick?" Saida asked me one evening after June had snapped at her for laughing too loudly at the television.

"Yes, baby. He's sick."

"Can the doctors make him better?"

That was the question, wasn't it? Could anyone make him better? And if so, how? June refused to admit he had a problem, refused to seek help, refused to consider that his drug use was affecting anyone but himself.

I tried everything I could think of. I hid money, locked up valuables, and watched him constantly.

I pleaded, argued, bargained, and threatened. I bought books about addiction, called hotlines, and looked into treatment programs. I enabled and then tried to stop enabling. I set boundaries and then let him cross them when he promised to change. Nothing worked.

June was drowning right in front of me, and every time I threw him a lifeline, he pulled me deeper into the water with him.

Letting Go

"You need to leave," I told him the next morning.

We were sitting on my front porch, drinking coffee, watching the Georgia sunrise paint the sky in shades of gold and pink. It should have been peaceful, brotherly, the kind of moment I'd dreamed of when I first invited him to come stay with me.

Instead, it felt like I was sentencing someone to death.

"Janet—"

"No. Listen to me. I love you. I will always love you. But I can't let you destroy my children's sense of safety in their own home."

"I'm getting better. I just need more time."

"You're getting worse, June. And you're taking us down with you."

The conversation that followed was brutal. June alternated between promises, threats, and tears. He accused me of abandoning him, of not caring about family, of being selfish and ungrateful. He reminded me of all the times he'd protected me as a child, all the ways he'd been there for me when I needed him.

All of it was true, and none of it mattered. Because the person who'd protected me, who'd been there for me, who'd loved me unconditionally, that person was disappearing a little more each day.

He was consumed by something stronger than our shared history, stronger than love, stronger than the bonds that had once made us JanetandJune.

"Where am I supposed to go?" he asked finally.

"I found a halfway house in Atlanta that has a bed available. They have programs, counselors, people who know how to help with this." "I don't need help. I need my family." Your family needs you to get help." He left that afternoon with the same duffel bag he'd arrived with six months earlier.

I helped him fill out the paperwork and hugged him goodbye like I was releasing him into the unknown.

"I'll call you every day," I promised.

"No, you won't," he said, and his smile was so sad it broke something in me. "But that's okay. You've got to take care of your own."

Brook's Story

If June's addiction was a wildfire, fast, destructive, impossible to ignore, then Brook's alcoholism was more like a slow flood, rising gradually until it drowned everything in its path.

Brook had always been a drinker. Growing up, that wasn't unusual in our family or our neighborhood. Men drank beer after work, wine with Sunday dinner, whiskey when they were celebrating or mourning, or just trying to get through another day.

Brook could hold his liquor better than most, never seemed sloppy or out of control, just loose and happy and more talkative than usual. But after our Mother died, something shifted. Casual drinking became regular drinking and became necessary drinking. Brook needed a beer to start his morning, a few more to get through his workday, and a bottle of something stronger to help him sleep at night.

His wife Mimi tried to manage it at first. She'd hide bottles, water down his whiskey, make excuses to friends and family when Brook missed social events or showed up too drunk to function. But managing an alcoholic is like trying to hold back the ocean with your bare hands—exhausting, impossible, and ultimately futile.

The call came from my brother Eric in Omaha on a Thursday evening in March, several months after June had left my house.

The details came out slowly. Brook had lost his job in Philadelphia, lost his apartment, and been asked to leave several friends' couches. Mimi had finally reached her limit and filed for separation, changing the locks and telling Brook he couldn't come home until he got sober.

Eric, who had moved to Omaha NE, and his wife Wendy had taken Brook in out of family loyalty, but their small house couldn't accommodate a functional alcoholic indefinitely. Especially not with twin toddlers who needed stability and quiet.

"He's not mean or anything," Eric assured me. "Just... sad. And drunk. All the time."

I said "no". My house was calm again, my children were relaxed, and my finances were stabilized. The last thing I needed was another brother's addiction disrupting our lives.

But this was Brook. My protector, my defender, the brother who'd always had my back no matter what. The one who looked like me, who shared my sense of humor, who'd made me feel special and loved from the day I was born. How could I turn my back on him when he needed me?

"Drive him down," I said, hating myself even as the words left my mouth. "But Eric he can't stay long. A month, maybe two, while we figure out treatment options." It was a lot. Too much. But family is family, even when family is slowly killing itself with bottles and pipes and the kind of pain that makes people choose numbness over healing.

Brook arrived on a Saturday in a U-Haul truck filled with the remnants of his adult life. Boxes of clothes, a few pieces of furniture, and photograph albums chronicling happier times. Eric helped unload everything into my garage, already crowded with Kenny's abandoned belongings and the detritus of other people's fresh starts that never materialized.

My brother looked terrible. Brook had always been handsome, tall, well-built, with the kind of smile that could charm anyone into anything. But alcohol had carved deep lines into his face, yellowed his eyes, given him the shaky, uncertain movements of someone whose body was staging a constant rebellion.

"Hey, baby sister," he said, hugging me with arms that felt fragile despite their size. "Look at you, all grown up and living in the country."

 "Look at you," I said, trying to keep my voice light. "Still ugly as ever."

He laughed, but it turned into a cough that went on too long. "Some things never change."

But everything had changed, and we both knew it. The brother who'd once lifted me onto his shoulders to see parade floats, who'd taught me to drive in empty parking lots, who'd been my champion and protector that brother was still somewhere inside this broken man, but he was getting harder and harder to find.

The Pattern Repeats

Brook's alcoholism was different from June's drug addiction, but no less destructive. Where June became paranoid and erratic, Brook became sentimental and repetitive. He'd sit at my kitchen table for hours, nursing a beer and telling the same stories from our childhood over and over again.

The smell clung to him even when he wasn't actively drinking, a sour, desperate odor that followed him through my house like a cloud. The real problems started when Brook began disappearing during the day. He'd walk to the convenience store ostensibly to buy cigarettes or soda, but he'd return hours later with the tell-tale signs of a drinking binge: slurred speech, unsteady gait, that aggressive friendliness that alcoholics mistake for charm.

Had felt it myself during my darkest moments, after my parents died, during my failed marriages, in those awful hours when depression settled over me like a lead blanket.

Yes, there were times that I tried to fill it with alcohol myself, but I knew that this course of action would lead to my demise, just like it did to the rest of my family.

He was quiet for the rest of the drive home. That night, I heard him throwing up in the bathroom, his body rejecting the poison he'd been feeding for months. I wanted to help, but I'd learned from June that you can't save someone who's determined to destroy themselves.

The Breaking Point

The end came sooner than I'd expected. That's when I realized I was recreating the same chaotic environment I'd grown up in. My children were learning to tiptoe around adult dysfunction, to pretend unconscious uncles were normal, to manage their own anxiety and fear while the grown-ups in their lives fell apart.

I was perpetuating the cycle I'd sworn to break. The conversation was difficult but necessary. Eric and his wife weren't equipped to handle Brook any more than I was, but enabling his addiction wasn't helping him; it was just prolonging his suffering while spreading the damage to innocent bystanders.

Kenny and I arranged for Brook to enter a treatment program in Atlanta, one that specialized in alcoholism and depression. I helped him pack his belongings and drove him to the treatment facility in Atlanta that might be able to save him.

"I'm sorry," he said as we waited for his boarding call. "I know I fucked up your life."

"You didn't fuck up my life, Brook. But you're fucking up your own, and I can't watch anymore."

"I love you, baby sister."

"I love you too. Get better. Please get better."

But he didn't get better. The treatment program helped for a while. Brook called weekly to report on his progress, his counseling sessions, and his newfound clarity about the roots of his addiction. For six months, it seemed like we'd found the answer.

Then he relapsed. Then he relapsed again. Then he stopped calling, stopped returning messages, disappeared back into the bottle that offered temporary comfort but no real solutions.

The Lesson

Addiction isn't a moral failing or a lack of willpower. It's a disease, as real and devastating as cancer or diabetes. But unlike other diseases, addiction convinces its victims that they don't need treatment, that they can handle it alone, that the people trying to help them are the real problem.

You cannot love someone into sobriety. You cannot manage their addiction for them. You cannot sacrifice your own family's well-being to enable someone else's self-destruction, no matter how much you love them, no matter how much history you share, no matter how desperate they become.

The hardest lesson of my adult life was learning to say no to people I loved. To set boundaries that felt cruel but were actually merciful. To understand that sometimes the kindest thing you can do for someone is refuse to make their consequences easier to bear.

I thought I was being loving, supportive, and family-oriented. Instead, I was being codependent, trying to control outcomes I had no power over while neglecting my primary responsibility to protect my own children.

The guilt from those failures would follow me for years. The wondering if I'd done enough, said the right things, and found the right treatment programs. The question was whether I'd given up too soon or held on too long. The terrible arithmetic of loss, two brothers gone, to addictions that claimed not just the addicts but everyone who loved them.

But I also learned something valuable from watching June and Brook destroy themselves: you can only save yourself. Everyone else has to do their own work, make their own choices, and find their own reasons to live instead of die.

It took me years to stop feeling guilty about putting my children's needs before my brother's addictions. But that guilt was the price of breaking the cycle of refusing to teach Sean and Saida that adult dysfunction was normal, that managing other people's problems was their responsibility, that love meant enabling self-destruction.

Some lessons you learn the hard way. Some boundaries you set through tears. Some love you express by letting go. And sometimes, saving yourself is the most radical act of all.

YOU MAKE ME FEEL

---

*F*eeling Like A Natural Woman

Before the day I met you, life was so unkind, you're the key to my peace of mind, you make me feel like a natural woman – Aretha Franklin

Jon King

I had gotten everything backwards, and I knew it.

On an ordinary day, I met a tall, broad-shouldered, handsome man in the Blockbuster video and we became fast friends. We began a love affair that lasted over 25 years. He became my anchor, my lifeline. I was determined to make a go of it. While problems marched on, I continued to see Jon. I was fascinated, traumatized, and in love. A grown ass woman, mother of two, and in love for the first time in my life, under tough circumstances no less.

At age 30, Jon was a full-grown man. He had been raised by his grandmother and was strong, self-supporting, and independent.

Jon bought me a pager, so we could stay in touch. Cell phones had not been invented yet. He became the only bright spot in my life, while I struggled like hell to dig myself out of a very deep hole. Jon began taking me to expensive restaurants, my nights were filled with passion and $200.00 meals, a big deal in the 90's.

Jon called when he said he would. He showed up on time for our dates. He opened doors, paid for dinner, and asked questions about my life like the answers actually mattered to him. After years of men who treated dating like a game they were trying to win, Jon's straightforward approach was refreshing and slightly unnerving.

Our first dinner was at a steakhouse in Buckhead, the kind of place with cloth napkins and wine lists I couldn't pronounce. I'd purchased a gorgeous but simple cocktail dress and spent twenty minutes in the bathroom mirror trying to look like I belonged in such a nice restaurant.

"You look beautiful," Jon said when he picked me up, and something in his voice told me he wasn't just being polite.

Over dinner, he told me about growing up without his parents, being raised by his grandmother, who worked two jobs to keep him fed and clothed and out of trouble.

"What kind of something?" I asked.

"A business. A reputation. Something that can't be taken away because someone else changes their mind about you."

I understood that desire for security, for building something solid that couldn't be swept away by other people's decisions or circumstances beyond your control.

"What about you?" he asked. "What are you building?"

The question made me pause. What was I building? For so long, I'd been focused on surviving, getting through school, raising my children, escaping bad relationships, and keeping my head above water. The idea that I might actually be building something positive, something intentional, hadn't occurred to me.

"A life where my children and I can be safe," I said finally. "Where they can dream about their futures without worrying about whether we'll have electricity next month."

Jon nodded like that was the most sensible goal in the world. "That's good work. Important work."

Nobody had ever called my parenting "work" before, let alone important work. Men had complained about my children, tolerated them, or tried to discipline them, but Jon was the first to recognize that raising them well was an achievement worthy of respect.

For the first time in years, I was excited about the possibility of letting someone into my life instead of just bracing myself for the inevitable disappointment.

Our relationship took on a deeper hue. We talked late into the night about our dreams and goals, and put them into motion. Jon bought a limousine, the first of many. I went to paralegal school at night and continued paying all the bills at home, while working a full-time day job. We set up an LLC., and we were off and running.

The Difference

Jon was different from Jeff, Billy, and Kenny in ways that went beyond surface characteristics. Where other men had promised things they couldn't deliver, Jon under-promised and over-delivered. Where others had been threatened by my independence, Jon seemed to respect it. Where others had treated my children as obstacles to overcome, Jon understood they were central to who I was and what my life looked like.

He didn't rush anything. We dated for several months before he met Saida. Sean was out of the house at the time after successfully completing an apprenticeship at Job Corps in Kentucky. Sean wanted to be a welder like Jeff. He was pretty good at it. Instead of trying to be her friend or father figure, Jon was simply himself: polite, interested in their lives, respectful of their relationship with me.

I found it almost disorienting. I kept waiting for the other shoe to drop, for the reveal that he was secretly broke or emotionally unavailable or addicted to something that would eventually destroy us both.

Instead, Jon was exactly what he appeared to be: a grown man who'd done his own work, faced his own demons, and emerged with the kind of centered confidence that can only come from knowing yourself and being comfortable with what you find.

"You're waiting for me to disappoint you," he said one evening as we sat on his couch after dinner, his arm around me as we watched a movie.

"What makes you say that?"

"The way you flinch sometimes when I make plans for next week, like you don't quite believe I'll still be here."

He was right, and his observation stung because it forced me to confront how damaged I'd become, how my expectations had been lowered by years of men who'd taught me that promises were just words and consistency was too much to ask for.

"I'm sorry," I said. "It's not about you. It's about—"

"The men who came before me," he finished. "I know. But Janet, I'm not them. I'm not going to disappear when things get complicated. I'm not going to make promises I can't keep. And I'm sure as hell not going to punish you for having standards."

The conversation that followed was unlike any I'd ever had with a romantic partner. Jon wanted to understand my boundaries, my fears, my non-negotiables. He asked about my children's needs, my career goals, and my dreams for the future. He listened without trying to fix everything, without minimizing my concerns, without making my past trauma about his ego.

"Here's what I can promise you," he said finally. "I can promise to be honest about what I can and can't do. I can promise to treat you and your children with respect. I can promise that if I ever decide this isn't working for me, I'll tell you directly instead of just disappearing or making you guess."

Those weren't the passionate declarations of eternal love I'd gotten from other men, but they were better than poetry. They were practical promises from someone who understood that real love was built on reliability, not just chemistry.

Building Something Together

By the end of our first year together, Jon and I had settled into something that felt both exciting and stable, a combination I hadn't known was possible. He had his own life and interests. I had mine, but we'd found ways to weave them together without losing ourselves in the process.

We started talking about the future — not in the vague, fantasy way I'd dreamed with previous partners, but with specific, achievable goals. Jon wanted to expand his limousine business. I was interested in possibly going to law school eventually, or at least advancing to a senior paralegal position, which I did.

We talked about traveling together, about the kinds of experiences we wanted to share, about what we each needed to feel fulfilled and secure. Jon had never been married, never had children, but he didn't see my kids as baggage to be tolerated, besides they were both adults.

But Jon wasn't Kenny or Billy or Jeff. He wasn't asking me to take care of him or manage his problems or sacrifice my goals for his convenience. He was offering to build something together, to combine our strengths instead of just merging our needs.

That night, as I lay in bed thinking about the future Jon and I might create together, I realized I'd finally learned the difference between settling and choosing. Settling was accepting less than you deserved because you didn't believe anything better was possible. Choosing was recognizing when someone offered you exactly what you needed and having the courage to say yes.

For the first time in my adult life, I was choosing rather than settling. And that choice felt like the beginning of everything I'd been building toward since I'd left Philadelphia in search of something better.

Jon King wasn't perfect, and neither was I. But we were perfect for each other in the ways that mattered, compatible in our values, complementary in our strengths, committed to building something that could last, not because it was easy, but because it was worth the work.

After years of relationships that felt like drowning, I'd thought I had finally found someone who knew how to swim alongside me instead of pulling me under. Someone who understood that real love wasn't about rescue or completion, but about partnership and growth and the daily choice to keep building something beautiful together.

It had taken me twenty years, three failed relationships, and countless heartbreaks to understand what healthy love actually looked like. But now that I'd found it, I was never going back to anything less.

Things went well between Jon and me for almost a year. During that time, my daughter, Saida, at age 20, got pregnant while away at school. I was stunned, not a sorry repeat of my own troubled life. Where did I go wrong? The last thing I needed was a brand-new child to raise. I was just starting to spread my wings, and now another baby. I was devastated. I told Jon the whole story.

Jon bought a limousine business (the first of many), and I helped him set up his LLC. His business was growing. He'd gotten contracts for a doctor whose patients wanted special treatment and for celebrities (mostly rappers), who wanted to avoid the press and groupies.

My paralegal career was also advancing. The law firm where I worked had recognized my organizational skills and attention to detail, and I was being assigned to increasingly complex cases. The work was challenging in a way that made me feel intellectually alive, and the steady paycheck was allowing me to build real financial security for the first time in my adult life.

Jon understood the demands of my career without feeling threatened by my success. When I had to work late on an important case, he'd pick up dinner for us. When I got a raise, he celebrated with me instead of finding ways to diminish my achievement.

"I'm proud of you," he'd say, and mean it completely.

I was shocked when he told me weeks later that he had found someone whom he could marry and have kids with. He didn't want to be tied down to a house full of someone else's babies, much less grandbabies. After all, he was only 30 years old.

Here I was at 36, with half-grown kids no less. This would never work. We were worlds apart. Suddenly, my carefully crafted world disintegrated, dissolved right before my eyes. I was heartsick. Although I understood, I was deeply hurt, rejected, and alone... again.

Several months went by without Jon's presence in my life. He contacted me many times to ask if we could pick up where we had left off. I was wary and uneasy. Heartbreak was becoming too familiar; I decided that I could do without it. After about a year, I finally gave in. I said yes, and we got back together.

I was very much in love, this time with a real adult. I cherished our time together. He continued to shower me with gifts, love, and affection. He was also a very skilled handyman, installing a ceiling fan and new tile floors. It felt wonderful to have someone who could say, "I'll take care of that," and actually do it. For the first time in my life, I felt safe with a man.

I introduced Jon to my new friend, Brenda Marten, who developed a crush on him, but I thought nothing of it at the time. Brenda and I double-dated with Jon's friend Chris. We went on weekend trips to the lake house owned by his boss.

We ate at great restaurants and went to live shows. I saw legendary artists like Janet Jackson and Little Richard (the father of rock and roll). This was the lifestyle I could get used to. Up until now, I only dreamed about it — suddenly, it became my reality. Is this what happiness feels like? Once again, I jumped back in headfirst.

Paralegal School

I had recently started my first real job as a paralegal with an up-start real estate firm, CH&W Mgt. The pay was not great, but it was on the MARTA rail line, and I could attend paralegal school after work. I decided that if I couldn't afford to go to law school, I would become a paralegal instead.

The classes were taught by well-respected attorneys and judges with impeccable credentials. The school was considered the best in Atlanta and duly recognized in the legal community.

It was a year-long certificate program with high admission standards. A bachelor's degree was a prerequisite to admittance to the National Center for Paralegal Training. Once again, the angels smiled down on me. I was admitted to the school and was offered a low-interest loan to help pay tuition.

My days were often 16 hours long between work and school. I toughed it out and graduated at the end of the year. I discovered that I had a knack for comprehension and interpretation of the law. I excelled in my classes. I had finally found my vocation. I was on my way to a profession I loved.

Jail

As luck would have it, during my 4th week on my new job, I got a collect call from some jail in Kentucky; my son Sean was in jail for domestic violence, just like Jeff. He beat up his girlfriend/baby momma. (What baby?). Sean later denied that baby, Yunity, saying that she was not his child. Bail had been set, and he needed someone to bail him out and come to get him.

As if on cue, my depression returned with a vengeance, just as things went from bad to worse. Fortunately, Kenny still lived in Atlanta and had just purchased a new car. I asked him to drive me to Kentucky to pick up Sean. He helped with gas and a motel. He was always very kind to me when it came to helping our struggling little family. I will always be grateful for that.

When Sean was released, I slammed the jail door so hard that the whole building shook. During and after the hearing, I refused to speak to Sean. The judge was afraid to release him to my custody, as my rage was obvious. I was jumping up and down, screaming at Sean, and had to be restrained. Kenny had to sign the paperwork. I was furious, especially for a stupid ass reason such as this. Jeff and Janet all over again.

Here I was stuck with a useless replica of Jeff. This was the gift that keeps on giving. I was doomed.

As an adult, I wasn't too particular about having Sean back at home. He was disruptive at best, inconvenient to say the least. I laid down a few ground rules, with no long-distance calls, and no company being at the top of the list. By this time, Saida and I had buried our differences and were getting along just fine. She was still working at Taco Bell and was looking forward to a stint in college or the Job Corps. Time to leave the nest. Meanwhile, I was drowning in obligation and responsibility. I was determined to change that.

I was determined to get out of the rut of low-paying jobs and a lifetime of sacrifice. True to form, Sean's presence was disruptive and inconvenient. He did indeed make a slew of long-distance calls, running up the phone bill to more than $500.00. I just happened to open the bill early one morning before going to work. When I saw the amount due, lots of long-distance calls, I was furious. I woke him up, yelling about the bill. We got into an argument. I kicked him out of my house on the spot. This event would begin a downward spiral that we never really escaped from. It was a harbinger of events to come.

Once again, my life was in turmoil for no fault of my own, or so I thought at the time. Remember, we are always, always responsible for the choices we make, always. Of course, the outcome is yours to define.... Always....

I learned to set firm boundaries and worked hard to clean up my act. I was still young, so there were no visible signs of the trauma I had endured. Soon, I was offered a paralegal position at a mid-size law firm in downtown Atlanta, after I left CH&W. Finally, I was able to pay bills. I even bought a good used car, a Honda. My finances were stable, and so was my home life. Everything was going well until my daughter informed me that she was indeed pregnant. I could not bear the thought of an abortion. She was 20 years old.

I reached out to my former mother-in-law, Jeanne (dubbed Nana by the kids). We remained close through the years. She gave me strong advice. "Don't let her step across that door seal with that baby. You'll be stuck forever if you let her stay at home with the baby." I agreed with her. By that time, Nana was making frequent trips to Atlanta to see the kids and hang out with me. Kenny was long gone, and Saida and I had the house to ourselves. In the meantime, Jon and I had reconciled, and my future seemed bright at last.

I found a rent-controlled 2-bedroom townhouse nearby and put Saida on the waiting list. I prayed that things would finally work out for me. It did. I even co-signed for the apartment and set about furnishing it. We went to thrift stores, Babies R Us, and other clothing outlets every weekend and began preparation for the new baby. Saida had a part-time job at Marshall's, which I shuffled her to and from. I was strapped, but forged ahead anyway. If she wanted to "buy the farm" and struggle as a single mom, fine, so be it. I accepted the challenge. I was motivated. It was 1998.

My adorable grandson, Elijah, was born on November 4, 1998. He had Billy's beautiful, sparkling, big brown eyes. I was delighted. I had enough income, which allowed me to grant my daughter a rather lengthy maternity leave, remembering how tough it had been for me when she and Sean were born.

I made sure my daughter and grandson wanted for nothing so that she could ease into this new role as a mother, without the hardships I endured. In short, I shouldered the bills. My daughter had a fully furnished townhouse, complete with a decked-out nursery with a rocking chair.

The baby's father and his family contributed to his care. The family loved, accepted, and supported my daughter and adorable grandson. Elijah looked almost exactly like his grandfather, Billy, which tickled the hell out of me.

Patricia Anne Harrell — Age 60

I also became good friends with the father's parents, a nice middle-aged couple, Patricia (Anne) and Edd Harrell. Later, I was told by Anne that my daughter told them that I had put her out in the street because I had a boyfriend.

Actually, there was some truth to that. But she was never put out of my home. The fact was that neither Jon nor I wanted to begin raising a family. There were trips to the beach, vacations, and long afternoons in bed, and plans for the future to be made.

Anne and I remained close friends for several years, enjoying many family celebrations and the shared joy of our grandchildren, until her premature death from kidney disease.

NO SAFETY NET TO CATCH ME

E nter the Dragon – Act I

A heavenly visit from Mom Mom

Sometimes I feel like a motherless child, a long way from home
- Traditional Spiritual

When Everything Falls Apart

The letter arrived on a Tuesday morning in April 2008, mixed in with credit card offers and utility bills, like it was just another piece of junk mail instead of a potential death sentence. I almost threw it away without opening it, another insurance company trying to sell me coverage I couldn't afford, or so I thought.

But something made me tear open that envelope, maybe the same instinct that had kept me alive through all the other disasters in my life. The letterhead was from Mutual of Omaha, the company where I'd bought life insurance years earlier on the advice of an agent who'd insisted I needed disability coverage too. He was right, I'm glad I took his advice.

"Based on your recent application for additional coverage, we regret to inform you that your blood work has revealed the presence of Hepatitis C antibodies..." The words blurred as I read them twice, three times, trying to make sense of what they meant. Hepatitis C. I'd heard of something drug users got from sharing needles, something that destroyed your liver, something that killed people slowly and painfully. Outside of that, I knew very little about the seriousness of a Hepatitis diagnosis.

But I'd never used drugs. Never shared needles. Never done anything that should have exposed me to this disease. How was this possible? The drug dealer boyfriend from twenty-five years ago, Jerry Carter, is dead now from stomach cancer while incarcerated. That had to be it.

That stupid, reckless relationship from my teenage years had followed me into middle age, a ghost from my past arriving to collect a debt I didn't know I owed.

The timing couldn't have been worse. The country was sliding into financial collapse, banks were failing, and the real estate market was crashing around us like a house of cards. Jon's limousine business was struggling as contracts dried up.

However, his finances were stable. I'd already been laid off from the law firm, along with half the legal support staff in Atlanta, as corporate clients cut costs and individuals could no longer afford attorney fees.

And now this. A potentially fatal disease with no insurance to cover treatment, no job to provide stability, and no safety net to catch me if I fall.

I entered my forties with renewed confidence, having secured a well-paying job as a senior paralegal in an upscale law firm in Midtown Atlanta. Remembering my family's sordid medical history and early deaths, I obtained life and disability insurance from Mutual of Omaha.

The agent strongly advised that I get a disability policy in the event of an unexpected illness or injury. Fortunately, I took his advice, which would prove to be the lifeline that protected me from the unseen dangers that lay ahead.

Several years later, I applied for additional insurance coverage to protect my growing family. My daughter had two small children by then, and I was all she had. Saida would have no one else if I died prematurely, like my parents before me had done, leaving them alone in the world with nothing.

Just to make matters worse, the country had a financial meltdown in 2008, largely due to poorly collateralized mortgages. I was unceremoniously laid off, along with millions of other Americans caught up in this ungodly mess.

By this time, I'd had over 10 years of professional experience in the legal industry under my belt. Fortunately, I was able to start my own paralegal company. I filed Pro Se bankruptcies and other Pro Se petitions in Magistrate Courts to keep money coming in. My company was fairly successful, and I was grateful for a way of helping people who were desperately trying to hold onto their homes.

Hepatitis C

I tested positive for Hepatitis C. This disease was contracted largely through unprotected sex with an infected person or the use of dirty needles. Apparently, my drug-using, drug-dealing boyfriend, Jerry Carter, had arrived from the past to kill me.

I only had three lovers in the past 20-plus years. I had never used hard drugs, and was at a total loss as to how I became infected with this deadly disease, except through Jerry, who used dirty needles to inject heroin as I would later discover.

Without health insurance coverage, I had nowhere to turn for medical help. Obamacare, or the ACA Act, simply did not exist at the time. Before Obamacare, insurance companies were not required to offer insurance if you had a preexisting condition, like cancer or hepatitis.

The Grady Health System is a local charity hospital that has had a hit-or-miss reputation at best. I entered a treatment program for Hepatitis C. The place was filled with junkies and homeless people. To say I was scared was an understatement.

The treatment plan was dangerous and had a poor success record. I continued on this treatment until it landed me in Piedmont Hospital in critical condition with double pneumonia. I was in the ICU for roughly over two months with no insurance.

Fortunately, my attending physician refused to let me be put out of the hospital, after 30 days... my life was in real danger. He called me his "baby", even though we were about the same age, and refused to let them release me until I regained my strength.

The hospital had no obligation to keep me there. I was on life support for two months. The hospital came to over $360.000.00. I had no insurance and no way to pay the bill. Losing my house was a real possibility.

I was in and out of a coma, and that's when it happened. My body was filled with a warm glow, and looking up, hovering over my bed was Mom-Mom. She was decked out in a golden cape and gown, which flowed beautifully around her. I watched as she floated around the ICU. She hovered over each machine that I was tethered to, as if to make sure they were working properly. Then she hovered over my bed, enveloping me in a soft, warm, golden glow, her gown flowing around her.

I received several messages from her, that I was going to be alright, and that she was watching over me. I was also told that I had inherited special privileges from Mom-Mom. Apparently, she had achieved a high ranking after her death. It was because of her status "over there" that my life was spared. During the next few days my private hospital room began to be filled with the distinct smell of her famous sweet biscuits.

Everyone who came into the room, visitors, nurses, doctors, technicians, all noticed that strong, sweet smell. I knew this was no accident, and my precious Mom-Mom was indeed standing by. With that knowledge, I was able to begin my recovery with renewed confidence and strength.

A few families and friends did come to visit me, including Kenny's son Seitu, notably missing was my own son Sean, who did not bother to show up from New York. Additionally, my brother June, who was living in a halfway house in Atlanta, while still trying to beat his drug addiction, after over 20 plus years, he too did not bother to show up. Brook was living in Newport News, VA, and still struggling with alcoholism. He, too, was unable to come.

My older brother James had died unexpectedly a few years earlier in Columbus, at age 59, and was obviously unable to show up. Brook did send me a little money, but was unable to come either. Brother Eric, now living in Omaha, Nebraska, with a horde of children, did not respond at all.

I was deeply shaken. I had lost one-half of my body weight, was on oxygen, in a wheelchair, and unable to walk. I had no real help except my daughter, Saida, who had initially taken me to the emergency and was terrified. She had no one to care for my little granddaughter, who was only about 6 years old at the time. One of her old school friends showed up to take care of Gabrielle. Panicked Saida turned to my old friend Brenda Marten, who rushed in from Washington DC to help.

When I was finally released from the hospital, Nana came from Philly to help me. She was a retired surgical nurse who knew her shit. I will always be grateful to her and the "baby" Doctor who helped save my life. He referred to me as "his baby" and refused to discharge me after a month, which was hospital policy.

I could not walk or stand without assistance. I had lost half of my body weight and was too weak to stand, walk or drive. I was helpless. It took several months to regain my strength. I resumed my habit of walking, but it took a long time to regain my pace.

Previously, I had applied for Medicare and disability, but my claim was denied. As a paralegal, I used my skills to mount an Appeal. Once I obtained a hearing, I hired an attorney from Johnnie Cochran's firm to assist. Mr. Cochran was my hero, not because of the OJ Simpson case, but because he was a damn good attorney who made the impossible possible. I hired an attorney from his firm.

In the meantime, I drafted the necessary legal documents and prepared to go to court. I won on Appeal in the Spring of 2012 and began receiving disability benefits about 2 years later. My private disability insurance, purchased on a whim from a flirty Mutual of Omaha agent, saved my home while the Appeal slowly dragged through the federal court system. Finally, I had a (literal) leg to stand on.

I was determined to get back on my feet and took a job at Allstate Insurance as a licensed agent, later that year. I had obtained my insurance license in 2008 and wanted to put it to good use, which I did.

Another Miracle

The hospital physician informed me that there was no known cure for Hepatitis C, and the program had not been very success-ful among the black population. I was proof of that. He emphat-ically explained that due to my poor reaction to the standardized Hepatitis C protocol, I had little chance of recovery.

Since there was no known effective cure for this disease, my life expectancy was cut short to about 5 years. Additionally, my case would be reported to the health department, because my disease was terminal, communicable, and a danger to the general popula-tion, like AIDS.

The Diagnosis

Dr. Georgia Theriot was kind but direct as she explained what the blood work meant. Yes, I had Hepatitis C. No, there was no way to know exactly when I'd contracted it—the virus could lie dormant for decades. Yes, it was serious. No, there wasn't a cure, but there were treatments that might help.

"The good news is that we caught it relatively early," she said, reviewing my test results. "Your liver function is still good, which means we have options."

"What kind of options?"

"There's a combination therapy of interferon and riboflavin. It's tough on the body, but it has about a 50% success rate for your genotype."

Fifty percent. A coin flip. Those weren't the kind of odds that inspired confidence, especially when she started describing the side effects: flu-like symptoms, depression, fatigue, nausea, hair loss, and anemia.

"It's basically chemotherapy for a virus," she explained. "We're going to make you very sick in order to make you well."

The treatment would take a year. A full year of feeling like I was dying in order to maybe, possibly, live. And that was if I could even afford it, which seemed increasingly unlikely as the bills started arriving.

Without insurance, the medications alone cost $3,000 a month. Add in weekly doctor visits, blood work, and monitoring, and the total was approaching my former annual salary. I'd spent years building financial stability, saving money, creating the kind of security I'd never had as a young mother. All of it would be gone within months.

"There are programs," Dr. Theriot said when I explained my situation. "Grady, the county hospital has a clinic for uninsured patients. It's not ideal, but they can provide the same treatment."

"Not ideal" turned out to be the understatement of the year.

Dr. Theriot continued to see me after my release from the hospital, even though I still had no insurance to pay her. She also met with other medical professionals and sought help for me in my battle to stop Hepatitis C from prematurely ending my life. Dr. Theriot referred me to a physician who specialized in liver disease, and I made an appointment.

Dr. Thelma Wiley-Lucas was a black female physician; she was exactly the right person at the right time. She too fought hard to save my life. Dr. Lucas enrolled me in a clinical trial for patients with chronic liver disease. Of course, this was not actually smooth sailing. The trail was free, but the medication was not. The prescription costs $1,500.00 per month.

Unbeknownst to me, Dr. Lucas entered me into a scholarship fund that covered the cost of the medication, and I was awarded full coverage. The notice came like a shiny Christmas gift through the mail. I was humbled, grateful, and broke out in loud, ugly tears at the mailbox. The program had a 98% survival rate, and I was one of a very select few who were fortunate enough to access this miracle drug, Harvoni. The drug is now widely available and continues to enjoy great success.

I am grateful to have been a part of a study that continues to save lives. Once again, God smiled down on me as he had done many, many times before. There was no doubt about his presence in my life.

My beloved Dr. Theriot was ill and kept her illness a secret until she was unable to continue working. Upon learning about this, I approached Dr. Bennett (who stepped in to help) and volunteered to help out until she recovered. Unfortunately, Dr. Theriot died in August 2019.

Broken-hearted I stayed with the new practice for several months. Once, when I was alone in the office, I felt her gentle presence of love and kindness. I lit candles around the reception area and attended her funeral, where I had to once again say goodbye to someone I deeply loved.

My heart was filled with gratitude for this gifted doctor who went above and beyond the call of duty. She literally saved my life. Every time I look at my grandchildren's smiles or walk down a street, I feel her presence, and my heart is full and grateful.

EXHALE

State of Emergency - Act 1

Brenda Marten Age – 64

Brenda Marten, a social worker and an old friend, and I stopped seeing "eye to eye" when she discovered that I had about $7,000.00 in the bank, while I was hospitalized, which I refused to part with. We had been close friends for over 20 years, taking vacations together, traveling across the country.

I trusted her with all my secrets, good, bad, and ugly. Saida called her in a panic when I was admitted to the hospital.

Yes, of course, I could help her, but I would not take on the responsibility of supporting her while I was fighting for my life. Incidentally, she had decided to come to Atlanta after she lost her job and her place. Previously, I would send money to her in DC, but she always needed more.

Eventually, she moved in briefly with me, under the pretense that she was there to help me after leaving the hospital. Later, she pleaded with Jon to let her stay with him, stating that my house was too remote (she had her own car).

Brenda later confided to me that she didn't want to stay at my house because she was afraid that I would die while in her care.

So, I was left home alone, very sick. Unfortunately, after she moved in with Jon, she began to gossip and spread rumors, which created suspicion and tension between Jon and me. At the time, we had been together for over 15 years.

Apparently, unbeknownst to me, Jon had taken up with another woman. Brenda conspired with Jon to keep her existence a secret.

As an old friend, I felt she should have told me that Jon certainly wouldn't admit it. I confronted her about it when I found out years later, after my recovery.

She made excuses, stating that I was sick and she didn't want to make matters worse.

My intuition told me something was going on; I knew something was wrong. In fact, Brenda had plenty of time, given that it had been several years since my recovery. She had plenty of time to tell me the truth, but chose not to.

Her disloyalty, outright lies, and manipulation broke my heart. It tore Jon and me apart.

Unfortunately, Brenda died before we had the opportunity to rekindle our relationship, which I was fully open to.

A mutual friend called to tell me the sad news. I reached out to her daughters and sister to share memories and offer my condolences. I will always love and miss her.

The Straw – Jon King 2

During my convalescence, our sex life was nonexistent. My intuition told me that he was messing around on me. I didn't need Brenda or anyone else to tell me that. Early one morning, Jon called to tell me that a co-worker had died from a drug overdose.

My mind flashed back to meeting a flirtatious white girl at his company's event. Then, I heard a voice say clearly, "Jon had something to do with her death". I tried to brush it off, but the thought would not go away.

After much digging and mediation, I learned the truth. Jon had been seeing this young girl on the side. He decided to end the relationship on Valentine's Day. He gave her a dozen roses and departed. The girl was later found dead, having overdosed the night before.

When I confronted him with the truth, he finally admitted it. This young girl had lost her life for nothing, to a player who could run back home to momma (me) when things got too rough in the real world.

I decided then and there that I could no longer be with a man who was at least partially responsible for someone's death, apparently for no other reason than to feed his ego. This was the proverbial "straw"; I could not get past it.

Jon and I continued to remain good friends, but without sex. I decided not to risk another heartbreak and embrace myself, which I did. The thought of being alone no longer disturbed me. Although it hurt to let go, somebody had to take care of Janet; that somebody was me.

Tired of Fighting

It had been a very tough year so far. It was June 2015, and I was terrified. So far, both of my children (who were adults by then) had serious health issues at the same time. I had just recently returned from Connecticut, where Sean had been hospitalized with a massive stroke.

His entire right side was incapacitated. He could not walk or speak clearly. We were on the phone when the stroke occurred. I instructed him to call 911. At the time, I/we didn't realize that it was a stroke after all; he was only 43 years old... this can't be!

When I arrived in Connecticut a few days later. Sean was in an awful mood, had no insurance, and had alienated the hospital staff. They were anxious to get him out of there. The good thing was that he was at Yale, with some of the best physicians in the country. Sean had no insurance to pay for his mounting hospital bills.

I brought my laptop along and got busy, applying for emergency Medicare, and smoothing the ruffled feathers of the frustrated staff. I worked closely with the social worker there and got him the help he needed to get his hospital bills covered. My brother June, had sent along enough money for me to stay at a local hotel near the hospital for about a week.

Sean was bitter and angry, yelling and cursing at everyone, yes, including me, which infuriated me. I rebuked him and reminded him that this is a direct result of his not taking an interest in his own well-being. I left the hospital in a huff, vowing to keep my ass out of hot water, especially when it came to my son.

We had been having constant battles over his irresponsible be-havior for years. I was sick of the arguments and the disrespect.

The next day, I took a tour of Yale University, given by a pretty young coed on a beautiful spring day. I caught an Uber from the hotel and was stunned to see a picture of the first black graduate from Yale, at about the turn of the century.

Interestingly, I wandered away from the group and found his pic-ture at the very back end of a long hallway. I was shocked, but not surprised.

When I got back to the hotel, I called Sean's grandmother, Nana, still my mentor, foster mother, and close confidant. She, too, was disappointed with the way things turned out for Sean. In the meantime, the family was engrossed in finding him a place to stay while he recovered from the stroke.

Not surprisingly, his grandmother and father refused to take him in. Even though they lived less than 3 hours away in Philadelphia, they had a spare bedroom. Jeanne/Nana was a retired nurse, yet there was no help forthcoming from them whatsoever. Jeff did visit Sean in the hospital once.

Sean was helpless with no place to go, except to my house, where I was currently recovering from a long hospital stay myself. How-ever, I was still willing, if not fully able, to help. I lived 1,000 miles away from him in Atlanta. In the end, Sean wound up staying with a friend in Connecticut. He had no money and no place to live after a long hospital stay.

Despite these encumbrances, we managed to keep him afloat. I stayed in constant contact with him, sending money and other resources whenever I could, until financial help arrived. I applied for and received emergency disability on Sean's behalf and advised him to move back to Atlanta pronto. The plan was to keep an eye out for him and prevent another disaster.

Eventually, Sean declined to come to Atlanta, preferring instead to move in with an old girlfriend in Florida. Later, there was a massive hurricane in Florida, and Sean was homeless, yet again. By then, we had not spoken for several months after a terrible argument while he was in the hospital.

I simply would not tolerate his nasty attitude and his refusal to hold himself accountable for his poor decisions. I offered him financial help, but would not allow him to move in with me.

Upon my return to Atlanta, from visiting Sean, about a week later, my daughter visited me and carefully explained that she had Stage 2, possibly 3rd stage breast cancer.

With a mother's love and sensitivity, I took my hand and put it right on the tumor, which was the size of a walnut! Apparently, she knew about this before I left for Connecticut.

She told her dad, and together they decided to conceal this fact until I returned. I was dismayed and felt betrayed. It took several months for a tumor of that size to grow without her being aware of its presence. Why hadn't she told me before now, when her very life was in imminent danger? It was the spring of 2015. I thought 2012 was rough. This takes the cake. What else could go wrong? I learned later not to ever ask that question again. This was becoming the worst year of my life. Saida was only 37 years old.

Because Saida's cancer was so aggressive and quickly advancing, her doctors advised her to begin weekly chemotherapy immediately. In the meantime, I had been working two part-time jobs. One as an Allstate agent and another at the local Target.

The staff there was very understanding, and I managed to be with Saida at every chemotherapy treatment and doctor's appointment. I climbed over the shrubbery, rocks, and grass to look through the window and make faces at her, while she withstood the grueling chemo treatments. Trying to make the unbearable, bearable.

Shortly after her cancer diagnosis, my daughter had unceremoniously moved into my house, without my knowledge or permission. I was on vacation visiting a friend in Colorado. I was not happy when I returned home to chaos. She only informed me AFTER she had moved in, on the day I was expected to return home.

Clothes everywhere, my house was a mess, total disarray, and smelled like a varsity football team's locker room. My designer clothes and shoes flung about. Bags of filthy, moldy clothes filled the garage with so much junk (washer, dryer, old furniture, and plain old trash), making it impossible to move about, let alone park my aging vehicle.

The privacy and independence I had worked so hard to achieve suddenly disappeared. Gone. My daughter had effectively checked out. Leaving the children for me to contend with virtually alone. I was deeply hurt by her decision to move into my house without notice, but under the circumstances, I felt that I had no choice, so I didn't object too much. I got it.

I was struggling to be strong for her, but it was tearing me down, piece by piece. After all, I was her mother.

I had lived in my house comfortably for almost 10 years and never had to face anything like this before. The privacy and independence I had worked so hard to achieve suddenly disappeared. Gone. My man could no longer come to visit me and provide the much-needed support I so desperately needed. Sex was out of the question. I was too exhausted to come to him.

I closed down my home office and turned it into a bedroom so my daughter and granddaughter would have a comfortable place to sleep. A good friend of mine donated a queen-size bed along with sheets and comforters. Saida would need a clean, comfortable place to rest while she recovered from the rigors of chemo and surgery.

I asked her to purchase another TV after she broke the one I had given her several months before she moved in with me. Prior to that, she and my granddaughter camped out on the living room couch, which by then was truly ready for the trash dump.

My grandson occupied the guest bedroom. I was in no position to take on additional responsibilities. I was deeply hurt by her decision to move into my house without notice. To be honest, her situation was a reflection of a series of bad decisions she'd made. Everybody makes mistakes, I understood that.

Due to her refusal to take or receive professional advice, her husband had been deported to his native Honduras and was unable to contribute to his family's support. Eventually, I had to leave my job at Allstate. As an independent agent, I no longer had a place to conduct business.

My office equipment had been either damaged, discarded, or destroyed, all by accident, of course. I had left the office equipment, along with my beloved printer, on a table in a corner of her bedroom, hoping that I could work in that little corner I had left. My bedroom was too small and lacked the connections for my office equipment. I did eventually replace the equipment and office furniture, but it was only after they moved out, almost 18 months later.

I felt that I had little choice but to push hard to get things done in order to keep the household running smoothly. Of course, I objected, but it only caused more arguments and friction in my house.

My home, my only refuge, suddenly became a boiling cauldron of resentment, nasty gossip, and painful discord. I was miserable. Prior to that, at least at home, I had some measure of peace. Not anymore.

After all, I was her mother, a position I believe she took for granted. Nevertheless, I pitched in and did the best I could under the circumstances. Household chores were primarily my responsibility. When I asked her to have the children, make up the bed, make them stop throwing trash on the floor, pick up behind themselves, basic stuff, it would turn into an argument, so I stopped asking.

She would pitch in occasionally, but I was careful not to push it. Believe me, I get it. Sometimes life can be so unfair, so harsh, that there comes a time in everyone's life to stand tall and face the music. Ready or not. Period.

I routinely began sifting through mounds of moldy or dirty clothes, picking out whatever I could find, so the kids would have clean clothes to go to school in. Later, she let me know on no uncertain terms that I should not continue this practice. I ignored her and continued to wash my grandchildren's clothes anyway.

I had offered to pay her rent, security deposit, moving expenses, etc., from what was left of my 401K money, shortly after she returned to work. Unfortunately, after she returned from work, she steadfastly refused to honor her promise to move out, even after she had finally recovered. I asked her to move out during the summer so the kids could change schools without too much difficulty.

I gave her full access to my resources, offered to pay her deposit, and even wrote a rental reference to help her relocate. I was still working at Target, so I was able to take advantage of sales and discounts. I even bought household necessities, like microwaves, dishes, mops, brooms, trash cans, you name it. I boxed up her belongings, now permanently located in my garage, most of which she later abandoned.

I believe she took my actions personally, and indeed, they were very personal. I wanted my house back. I wanted my life back. I truly believed that I'd gone over and above the motherly 'call of duty'. It was time to break camp.

Despite the fact that I'd worked tirelessly to help her, she refused to speak to me for several years afterwards. We have since buried the hatchet and enjoy a good relationship today.

WHAT ELSE CAN GO WRONG?!

The Hammer - ACT III

Later, that same year, I went in for my yearly mammogram, and the hammer dropped. The hospital called and told me that they found "something". I was asked to come in immediately for a biopsy. I remember thinking, 'what the fuck is 'something' for some reason, it didn't occur to me that I might have breast cancer.

After the biopsy, I called Dr. Theriot and asked her to please look into this for me, which she did. I did the monthly self-exams faithfully, and hadn't felt a thing. Cancer, not a chance.

I was really taken aback by the way I came about my breast cancer diagnosis. Looking back, I should have known something was up. It all began with a routine visit with my PCP, Dr. Georgia Theriot.

We were about the same age and had become very good friends over 10 years that I'd known her.

She would always fuss at me about getting my yearly mammogram. I remember thinking, " This time I'm fixing her smart butt'. I'll have the mammogram results before my Dr. visit, so I can laugh at her for nagging me so much.

Dr. Theriot had a good friend in pathology who was kind enough to process my tissue sample immediately. The results came back the next day. I had confirmation of my worst fear. I did indeed have breast cancer, Stage I.

The cancer was less than 1 cc, too small to feel with my bare hands, but cancer nonetheless. The peculiar thing about this was that it all started from my desire to make fun of my doctor. Without it, things may have gotten a lot worse before it was discovered.

We need to get you to a doctor immediately." The next twenty-four hours were the longest of my life. I couldn't eat, couldn't sleep, couldn't focus on anything except the possibility that I might have passed a death sentence to my child through my DNA.

What was the point of surviving my own medical crises if I'd condemned my daughter to face the same battle?

When Saida called with her results, I was prepared for the worst. The reality was somehow both better and worse. Mother and Daughter, Patient and Patient. genetic testing confirmed what we'd suspected: BRCA1 positive. A defective gene that dramatically increased our risk not just for breast cancer, but for ovarian cancer, the disease that had killed my mother at age fifty-three.

Dr. Sroka explained the numbers with clinical precision that somehow made them more terrifying: 87% lifetime risk of breast cancer, 44% risk of ovarian cancer. For women with BRCA1 mutations, the question wasn't whether they'd develop cancer, but when and how aggressive it would be.

"The good news," she said, "is that we know what we're dealing with. We can be proactive instead of reactive. We can make decisions based on data instead of just hoping for the best."

The data was stark. For Saida, who'd already developed breast cancer at thirty-eight, the recommendations were clear: aggressive treatment followed by prophylactic mastectomy and eventual removal of ovaries and fallopian tubes.

For me, approaching fifty, the calculus was different, but the message was the same this gene was a loaded gun, and we needed to act before it fired again.

"What about my granddaughters?" I asked.

"They can be tested when they're old enough to make informed decisions. If they carry the gene, they'll have options we didn't have: better screening, preventive surgery, targeted medications. Knowledge is power when it comes to hereditary cancer."

Knowledge is power. But knowledge is also a burden, the weight of understanding that your family line carries invisible danger, that every woman who shares your DNA faces the same terrible lottery.

The fact of the matter was that both my daughter and I had breast cancer at the same time. We needed to get to the bottom of this immediately. The doctors suspected that this was probably hereditary. My mind was racing with fear, would my child and I survive, would my granddaughters get cancer too? How could this have been avoided?

In despair, I called the local hospital in Fayetteville, GA, and stated, "Please give me the baddest SOB you've got". I've just been diagnosed with breast cancer, and I need a badass to help me ASAP. That's how I met Dr. Sroka, the "Boss."

I made an appointment with Dr. Nicole Sroka, a skilled breast surgeon and a graduate of NY Sloan-Kettering, who was considered the best in her field. Upon meeting her, I gained full confidence that we would be able to beat this thing. Saida met me at the appointment, and I was grateful for her presence.

Through tears, I explained that both of us had a recent breast cancer diagnosis and would need to coordinate our efforts and create a dual treatment plan if this endeavor was going to be successful. Saida had just completed her chemo regimen, and her next step was radical surgery. However, I, too, had to have surgery and soon. Because my tumor was considerably smaller, Dr. Sroka and I decided to do my surgery first, then chemo afterward.

Surgery was scheduled for both of us at different hospitals, in the same month of October 2015. My surgery was scheduled for the first week. Saida's surgery was scheduled for the last week of October, coincidentally 'breast cancer month'. Hopefully, I will have a little time to recover from my surgery and help my daughter.

However, due to the advanced stage of her cancer, it was recommended that Saida undergo a double mastectomy. Saida had to face losing both breasts at 38, a damn tough pill to swallow for someone so young. Understandably, she was deeply depressed and in terrible shape.

Those were trying times indeed. I had to face the possibility that I, too, could die from breast cancer, while my only daughter was at an even greater risk, given that her cancer was much further advanced. There is nothing more challenging than having to face your own mortality while facing the fact that your daughter was confronting the same damn thing at the same time.

I checked in for my surgery in early October 2015, a lumpectomy. Dr. Sroka advised that the surgery would be outpatient, and I could go home the same day if I didn't have any complications. Fortunately, breast cancer surgery has come a very long way since my mother's time.

My mom had a sister, Ruth, who had breast cancer surgery, which left a huge, nasty scar where her left breast had been. Given the way medicine was practiced back in the 50's, I feel especially blessed that she survived at all. Aunt Ruth had a pivotal role in my family.

Most events like birthdays, weddings, and baby showers happened in her large, beautiful home at 32nd and Berks Street, near Fairmount Park. I remembered her scars and was terrified of what my daughter's breasts would look like after the surgery.

My surgery was a big success. Dr. Sroka had gone through my armpit and plucked the tumor out, a breeze. I was both relieved and amazed at her skill as a surgeon. I had 3 weeks to recover before Saida's scheduled surgery at the end of the month.

She was to have a double mastectomy, plus reconstructive surgery, a procedure that would take over 16 hours. I asked one of my friends from Target, LaToya, to look out for my 7-year-old granddaughter, and I was off to the races to save my daughter's life.

The hospital was nearly 40 miles away from my home. Driving the back roads home was difficult and painful, having only recently gone through surgery myself, but I made it.

Although I was in almost constant contact with a few family members and friends, the fact of the matter was that I was in this all alone. Faith and prayer were my only companions. I was scared and lonely. Surely, things had to get better from here, and they did.

WE WIN!

The Road to Recovery

The road to recovery was difficult and complicated. Neither of us had the support we so desperately needed. Saida's husband had been deported a few years earlier due to Saida's refusal to follow or receive professional advice...and she was on her own. My man was juggling a full-time job and a business, a virtual albatross, so I get it, but it didn't help things.

One of my biggest fears was starting chemotherapy, something I wanted to avoid at all costs. I approached Dr. Sroka with the option of skipping the chemo treatments altogether, given that she had surgically removed the tumor. The problem she explained was that the cancer could come back, perhaps somewhere else in the body. The objective is to stamp it out and prevent new growth.

I cringed at the thought of losing my hair and forged ahead. These side effects are well-known, but become a much tougher reality to face when it's happening to you. Actually, I lost more than hair; my nails turned black and fell off as well. I looked funny, my ego took a beating and forced me to look deep inside myself to find the guts to fight back, against terrible odds. The chemo made me sick and nauseous, but I was given an on-board, time-released adhesive pod, which helped the symptoms a great deal.

I took 30 days leave of absence from work and Saida, and I began to 'slug it out', fighting cancer, fighting demons, fighting fear, and finally fighting each other. I dug in and went back to work at Target, which had become somewhat of a safe haven for me. I really enjoyed the people there and became friends with some of my co-workers.

Actually, the hours were perfect for my chemo schedule, which was every day for about 10 weeks. I would go to work at Target from say, 6:00 to 12:00, grab some lunch and begin chemo every afternoon. Usually, I try to get back home before my granddaughter returns from school. My old friend at the time, Brenda Marten, would call after she returned from Washington, DC to help coach me through my anger and frustration at being forced into such an untenable situation. Sometimes, I did very well; other times, I failed miserably, with visions of what my life would be like without this terrible chain of events. What happened? Did God not love me anymore? I felt so lost, adrift.

Obviously, getting to the root of this disease was paramount. It was no accident that we both, mother and daughter, wound up with breast cancer at the same time. Eventually, we took the BRACA1 exam made famous by Angelina Joelee. Her contribution to the conversation regarding DNA as one of the main factors in determining the chances of getting cancer was vital because it brought the discussion out in the open. While a healthy lifestyle can be helpful, it is not the only predictor of your chances of getting cancer; DNA, however, is.

I am truly grateful for the lives that have been saved, because now people have access to technology that can help shape decisions, which are vital to our chances of survival. It is critical to have the ability, knowledge, and resources to make hard choices when it comes to stamping out this terrible disease. For this, I am truly grateful.

The BRCA test revealed that I had a 97% chance of getting ovarian cancer, the cancer that killed my mother. My daughter had an 88% chance of getting it as well. A total hysterectomy was advised; she was just past 39 years old and was hoping for another child when her husband returned. I am proud of her strength and willingness to face some hard truths and come out victorious, some mean feat.

Waiting for the Other Shoe to Drop

Fighting for Life-Coordinating Our Battles

Saida's treatment was more intensive than mine, which was more than my six months of chemotherapy followed by surgery, then radiation. My treatment was surgical first a lumpectomy to remove the small tumor, followed by a shorter course of targeted therapy.

We became partners in survival, coordinating our medical appointments, sharing information about side effects and treatment options, and supporting each other through the physical and emotional challenges of fighting the same disease simultaneously.

The logistics were complex. Saida's children, my grandchildren, ages eight and ten, needed stability while their mother underwent treatment that would make her sick, exhausted, and emotionally fragile. Her husband, Manuel, was doing his best, but was in Honduras and had no means to help.

Jon stepped up in ways that made me fall in love with him all over again. "This is what family does," he said when I tried to thank him for the hundredth time. "We take care of each other."

But the strain was enormous. I was trying to be strong for my daughter while fighting my own cancer, trying to support my grandchildren while managing my own treatment schedule, trying to maintain some sense of normalcy while our family faced the possibility of losing two mothers at the same time.

Some days, I felt like I was drowning in responsibilities and emotions that I couldn't process. Other days, I felt grateful that my daughter and I could face this together, that neither of us had to fight alone.

The hardest part was watching Saida lose her beautiful hair. She'd inherited my mother's thick, lustrous locks, and seeing them fall out in clumps from the chemotherapy was like watching part of her identity disappear. "I look like an alien," she said one evening, running her hands over her bald scalp.

"You look like a warrior," I told her. "You look like someone who's fighting for her life and winning."

The Surgery Decision

After Saida completed her chemotherapy and her tumors had shrunk to an operable size, she faced the hardest decision of her life: lumpectomy or mastectomy. Given her BRCA1 status and the aggressive nature of her cancer, her oncologist recommended a bilateral mastectomy, removal of both breasts to eliminate the risk of recurrence.

She was thirty-eight years old. Still young, still beautiful, still defining herself partly through her physical appearance and feminine identity. The idea of losing her breasts was devastating, but the alternative, risking her children's future by leaving cancer cells behind, was unacceptable.

The surgery was scheduled for October, just weeks after my own lumpectomy. We'd be recovering simultaneously, helping each other through the physical healing while processing the emotional aftermath of having our bodies permanently altered by cancer.

The night before Saida's surgery, who inconsolable cried bitterly. I'm scared, Mom. What if I wake up and don't recognize myself? What if Manuel can't love me the same way? What if the kids are afraid of me?"

I knew those fears intimately. Cancer doesn't just attack your body, it attacks your sense of self, your confidence, your belief in your own future. It makes you question everything you thought you knew about strength and femininity and mortality.

"You're going to wake up alive," I told her. "Everything else is manageable. Everything else can be figured out. But alive is non-negotiable."

Recovery and Reconstruction

Saida's surgery took sixteen hours. Double mastectomy with immediate reconstruction, a complex procedure that removed all breast tissue while creating new breasts from tissue taken from her abdomen. She'd wake up with a completely different chest, extensive scars, and weeks of difficult recovery ahead.

I spent those sixteen hours in the surgical waiting room, praying to every deity I could name and making bargains with the universe. Take me instead. Let me absorb her pain. Give her a long, healthy, happy life, and I'll accept whatever comes next for myself. The recovery was brutal but manageable. Saida couldn't lift anything heavier than a coffee cup for weeks, couldn't drive, and couldn't shower without assistance. The new breasts were numb and would remain so permanently, a trade-off for cancer-free survival.

But she was alive. The pathology report showed that the chemotherapy had destroyed most of the cancer cells, and the remaining tissue was clear of malignancy. The genetic testing had revealed the enemy, and we'd defeated it before it could spread.

The BRCA Decision

Soon after Saida's surgery, I faced my own BRCA-related decision. My cancer had been successfully treated with a lumpectomy, but the genetic testing showed I had a 97% chance of developing ovarian cancer, the same disease that had killed my mother.

The recommendation was prophylactic removal of ovaries and fallopian tubes, a procedure that would eliminate the cancer risk but throw me into immediate menopause. Now in my fifties, I had hoped to approach menopause naturally, but surgical menopause would be abrupt and potentially more difficult to manage.

The decision wasn't difficult. I'd watched my mother die from ovarian cancer and seen the devastation it brought to our family. I'd seen what advanced cancer could do to someone I loved. If removing my ovaries would prevent my grandchildren from watching me die the same way I'd watched my mother die, the choice was obvious.

The surgery was outpatient, minimally invasive, nothing compared to what Saida had endured. But the emotional weight was enormous, another piece of my identity as a woman, another body part sacrificed to the God of cancer prevention.

"How do you feel?" my daughter asked as we drove home from the surgical center.

"Lighter," I said, surprising myself with the honesty of the answer. "Like I've been carrying a weight I didn't realize was there, and now it's gone."

The weight of genetic predestination, of inevitable disease, of waiting for the other shoe to drop. I'd spent my entire adult life wondering when cancer would come for me, and now I'd beaten it to the punch. I'd taken control of my genetic destiny in a way my mother and grandmother never could.

Lessons in Shared Battle

Fighting cancer alongside my daughter taught me things about love, strength, and family that I couldn't have learned any other way. We'd faced our deepest fears together and emerged stronger, closer, and more grateful for the time we had.

I learned that genetic predisposition isn't destiny, it's information. Information that can be used to make proactive choices, to catch problems early, to prevent tragedies before they occur. My mother didn't have the option of genetic testing, didn't know that her DNA carried hidden dangers. Saida and I had knowledge that saved our lives. I learned that medical advances happen faster than most people realize. The treatments available to us in 2015 were light-years ahead of what my Aunt Ruth had faced in the 1960s. Targeted therapies, genetic testing, reconstructive surgery, and supportive care, all of it designed to help women not just survive cancer, but thrive after it.

Most importantly, I learned that sharing a battle makes both fighters stronger. Saida and I supported each other through treatment in ways that neither of us could have managed alone. We took turns being strong when the other was weak, celebrated small victories together, and faced our fears with the knowledge that we weren't fighting alone.

The physical scars would fade, but the emotional bonds forged during those months of shared crisis would last forever. We'd looked death in the face together and chosen life, chosen each other, chosen to keep fighting no matter what our DNA tried to dictate.

A New Understanding

Ten years after our diagnoses, Saida and I were both cancer-free and thriving. She'd returned to work, and her children had adjusted to their mother's new appearance.

My relationship with Jon had deepened in ways that surprised me. Facing mortality together had eliminated any pretense or superficial concerns that might have lingered in our partnership. We'd seen each other at our most vulnerable and chosen to remain friends, to keep building a good relationship, despite the fragility of human existence.

But the experience had changed my perspective on everything. Medical crises, I'd learned, were like earthquakes; they shook everything loose that wasn't firmly anchored. Priorities became clear, relationships were tested, and what mattered most rose to the surface while trivial concerns fell away.

I no longer worried about small problems that had once seemed overwhelming. Financial stress, family drama, work disappointments, all of it paled in comparison to the simple miracle of being alive and healthy. I'd been given another second chance, and I wasn't going to waste it on things that ultimately didn't matter.

The genetic testing had also given us a gift beyond medical information; it had given us agency. My granddaughters would grow up knowing they carried the BRCA1 mutation, but they'd also grow up knowing they had options. Early screening, preventive surgery, and targeted treatments that hadn't existed for previous generations.

The family curse that had claimed my mother threatened me and attacked my daughter, would end with us.

We'd broken the cycle not through luck or prayer, but through knowledge, medical science, and the courage to make difficult decisions based on data rather than hope.

Some battles are worth fighting, and some wars can actually be won. Cancer had underestimated the strength of women who'd already survived everything life had thrown at them. It had picked the wrong family to mess with, and we'd proven that love, science, and stubbornness could triumph over even genetic predestination.

We were more than survivors; now we were victors. And that victory belonged not just to us, but to all the women in our family line who would benefit from the knowledge we'd gained and the choices we'd made.

The fight was over. We'd won.

THE RUN DOWN

L ive to Tell

A man can tell a thousand lies, I've learned my lesson well...Hope I live to tell the secrets I have learned, until then it will burn inside of me - Madonna

Over the recent years, I have continued to suffer great losses. In my opinion, most of the losses could have been avoided or outright prevented. Maybe it's just wishful thinking, but I think we'll all be a lot better off should we heed the voice of reason.

Although my efforts and constant warnings went unheeded, I had no choice but to stand guard over disaster after disaster. Lose by default if you will. Although these are people whom I dearly loved, unfortunately, I was unable to stop them from destroying their lives. I offer these stories as a cautionary tale in the hope that you will heed my plea and take decisive action to protect yourself and those you love.   That being said. This is the rundown.

I started this life with six brothers. I am now down to only two. Unfortunately, they are not particularly interested in what I have to say. Even in the face of these tremendous losses, they still refuse to change their self-destructive behavior or acknowledge the losses our family has endured. That being said. Here is the run-down.

Clarence Moore - Age 76

My brother Clarence was always affable, kind, and loving to me. He had a stutter and called me Ms. Janet. Clarence stopped drinking and smoking, which added a few years to his life. He was married to the same devoted woman, Edith, until her death in 2005. I visited him in Philadelphia when I heard he'd had a heart attack. I rushed to his side, although he lamented the fact that his brothers did not come to see him. I encouraged them, but they chose not to show up.

My young niece Christine, also diabetic, called me early one Sunday morning in 2014 to advise me of his passing. I was still in recovery from my own illness, exhausted, underweight, and weak. I showed up, with arms open wide to help his two children through their crushing grief. My beloved brother Booker T. and his lovely (estranged wife Mimi were both present. I needed their strength and was grateful for their presence.

My hands were steady; my eyes were clear and bright. My walk had purpose, my steps were quick and light. And I held firmly to what I felt was right. Like a rock. -Bob Seeger

James W. Moore -Age 59

James was a retired Army Vietnam War veteran who worked hard to stay in shape. In fact, it was because of him that I took up the lifelong habit of running, which eventually saved my life and keeps me active and healthy to this day. Uncle James, as the kids called him, was well over 6 feet tall with a broad chest and big, strong arms that encircled me often throughout my life.

I can never remember a time when he wasn't picking me up and carrying me around, a habit he continued long after I grew up. He was a committed vegetarian and was very cautious about his health. He took on the leadership role in the family after our mom died. Unfortunately, he (and perhaps his wife Jessie) decided on an elective surgery that took his life.

He disappeared rather suddenly from my life. Poof...gone forever. He died on the operating table. The wife lied about the cause of death and refused to hand over family heirlooms, left to James by my mother.

This included insurance policies on all his siblings as well as original birth certificates for all of his siblings. James had a beautiful portrait of my mother commissioned. His wife refused to return these items, stating that she did not want ME to have them. She had never met my mother. Our family was not invited to his house after the funeral, a long-standing tradition, which was denied due to her sick jealousy and the unresolved emotional issues that she harbored throughout her marriage to my brother.

Additionally, Jessie refused to probate his will (although James told me he had written one). Jesse kept any and all of James' possessions as well as insurance proceeds by not probating his Will. The proceeds of which were to be divided equally among his siblings, as James had stated to me many times.

I contacted an old attorney friend of mine, who stated that it was easier to just let the matter pass, rather than fight her in Probate Court. It was too much of a hassle, after all, it would not bring my beloved brother James back to me. Also, there was a matter of medical malpractice that later came to light.

He died from a medical mistake during an elective operation. But Jessie refused to bring the matter to an attorney, and thus, nothing happened to redress the matter of his premature death.

Jesse was aware of my brother's position as head of our family. His love and commitment to keeping his siblings together were ever-present. Yet his wife chose to ignore his wishes, disrespecting him in his final moments.

His wife was jealous, rude, and disrespectful to our entire family (not just me) before, during, and after the service. The funeral was awful. She stood in front of his casket and lied to the entire congregation, as I would later discover. I guess that was her chance to show what she was really made of. I never spoke to her again. James was a good man who didn't deserve such disrespect after he raised her 3 children from another marriage. In the end, we received none of my brothers' belongings. All of it was lost...

*Standing in the shadows of love... waiting for the heartache to come...*The 4 Tops

Robert Pinkney - aged 56

Robert was diagnosed with diabetes as a juvenile and placed on insulin at a very young age. Tall, stocky, charismatic, with a head full of wavy hair, he was dark and handsome. Robert had the uncanny habit of chasing me, throwing me down on the floor, tickling me, and covering me with kisses, until I cried "uncle" every time he saw me. How I loved being loved by him.

Robert was a shameless womanizer and had accumulated at least 3 wives. He was working on a 4th wife when his diabetes took a turn for the worse. He endured over seven amputations, often on the same or both legs. He lost all of his limbs but one, his left hand. Every other body part was amputated.

Robert kept getting infections due to the filthy conditions he was forced to live in. His wife, Amy, a spoiled, lazy woman, threatened to kick him out of the house if he continued to speak with me. She asked me to hire a maid. She did not want to clean up after Robert, who was bedridden and incapable of caring for himself.

They lived in Lebanon, Ky, but I made the trip biweekly to clean the house and often paid large electric bills (averaging about $500.00 dollars a month) created by Amy and her daughter. Robert was constantly in and out of the hospital. Something had to be done, so I stepped up, once again.

I drafted and had Robert sign a power of attorney, which allowed me to have Robert's medical records transferred to Atlanta. This was done to secure hospice care, given that his wife, Amy, was unable, unwilling, or just plain incapable of properly caring for him. I reached out to the appropriate state authorities, who showed up promptly to help.

Unfortunately, Amy forced Robert to abandon the extra medical help I obtained for him and discarded the cell phone I bought to keep in touch with him. At the end of his life, he was not permitted to speak to me, his children, or his siblings. Helpless and totally dependent on Amy, she would often threaten to throw him out in the street if he continued to speak to me or anyone in the family.

Meanwhile, the Power of Attorney was rendered useless. Robert chose to remain with his abuser, and this decision shortened his life. In his last hour, he begged Amy to let him speak with me over the phone. I listened while he took his last breath.

Interestingly, and yet unbeknownst to anyone else, Amy had already begun an affair with my brother, June, which by any measure was a disgrace. They were together both before and after Robert's death, they finally admitted. Shameful behavior to say the least. After the funeral, I caught the first plane out of Kentucky, checking out of the hotel well before sunrise and arriving back in Atlanta early that same morning.

In the clearing was a boxer and a fighter by his trade, and he carries the remainder of every glove that laid him down... I am leaving, I am leaving, but the fighter still remains – The Boxer – Simon & Garfunkel

Booker (Brook) T. Pinkney — Age 66

Brook's years of alcoholic abuse finally caught up to him in his mid-60's. His only child, a devoted daughter, Chanda, moved him into her home, but found it impossible to care for him. Eventually, he was placed in a nursing care home and died there during the Covid pandemic.

I visited him in the nursing home a few weeks before his sudden death. I was devastated. All these losses took place in a period of less than 10 years. His passing was particularly painful for me. I grieved constantly. The combined losses were insurmountable.

The nursing home was supposed to be temporary, just until he stabilized and could transition to a less intensive care setting. Instead, it became his final address, a sterile environment where he spent his last months surrounded by strangers instead of family. When COVID hit and the facility locked down, Brook became completely isolated from everyone who loved him.

No visitors, no family gatherings, no familiar faces to comfort him as his condition deteriorated.

No viewing. No visiting. No chance to say goodbye to the brother who'd taught me to tie my shoes, who'd defended me against bullies, who'd called me his "baby sister" even when we were both middle-aged adults with children and mortgages and complicated lives of our own.

The protective brother, the generous spirit, the person who'd made me feel safe in a world that often felt dangerous. I was aware that most people in had never known that version of Brook, had only seen the broken man he'd become in his final years.

The brothers who remain...

> *Don't worry, if there's a hell below, we're all gonna go.* -Curtis Mayfield

Willie J. Pinkney (June) Aged -73

June and I rarely speak to each other, nowadays, although he is very much alive. Too much water under the bridge. Losing our close relationship was akin to losing a right arm. His over 25-year addiction to alcohol, crack cocaine, plus constant trips to rehab facilities throughout Atlanta destroyed his peaceful persona and created a mean-spirited narcissist in its place. He has since moved back to Philadelphia to be near his children.

I intentionally avoid him to prevent conflicts and dodge his constant criticism of me to anyone who would listen, especially my children, who held him in such high regard. June still maintains his disloyal, disrespectful behavior towards me. I stopped trying to figure out why. My response is to remain polite, to in some way honor the caring, loving man he used to be, and show respect for the close bond we once shared.

> *Me and baby brother used to run together* - War

Eric Pinkney – Age 64

Eric was 5 years younger than me and was always tagging along behind. I teased him constantly about not being born a girl, but I was very protective of him. We shared many delightful moments together. He was only 18 when our mother died. I lovingly took him under my wing. He lived with Kenny and me for a few years before moving in with Brook when I left Philadelphia to move to Atlanta.

Eventually, Eric moved to Omaha, Nebraska, to be near his childhood sweetheart, Wendy. Together, they had two beautiful twins, Eric Jr. and Marketia Minerva (after my mother). Eric began an affair with a neighbor, Sherry, during which another child was born, Jonathan, the following year. Wendy was so devastated that she was unable to care for the twins alone.

Eventually, she gave over custody of the twins to Sherry and Eric, the woman who slept with her husband behind her back. Wendy then tried courageously to move on with her life. She even got along with Sherry, who took over her role as a mother. However, the wounds never truly healed. Wendy remained a woman in suspended animation.

Today, Wendy still commands a great deal of love and respect from the family, largely due to her role in Eric's life since she was a teenager.

Eric eventually married a promiscuous, overweight woman, named Auggie, whose family was deeply prejudiced and didn't hesitate to show it.

The wedding was a disaster; I wore my trusty little black dress as a silent sign of protest. I couldn't wait to get the hell out of there, which I did. Her family was openly rude and hostile. The role of a good wife can be transformative and enlightening. Unfortunately, his marriage had a devastating effect on Eric and his children, who were just entering young adulthood.

I'm sure he did his best to be a good father; however, over the years, his lack of presence in their lives was keenly felt. Maybe Auggie did actually have some good qualities, but they were difficult to pinpoint, given the co-dependent, self-serving dynamic of their relationship.

Of course, I spoke directly to Eric about this issue, citing the OJ. Simpson mess and how inter-racial relationships rarely work out, and what I feared for him going down that road. Unfortunately, he chose to ignore me and married her anyway.

Over the next few years, perhaps in part due to losing his beloved brothers, Eric slipped rapidly into isolation from the family and began to drink heavily. Once again, the downward spiral of alcoholism and the generational curses in my family were always waiting in the wings.

 Finally, Eric was involved in a drunk driving accident, which permanently crippled the other driver. He was sentenced to 5 years in prison. Angry and bitter, his wife divorced him while he was in prison and actually called me for sympathy. I was polite and supportive, but puzzled, given the way I was treated at her wedding. Eric is totally disabled after a debilitating stroke.

He now lives in a nursing home in Omaha, Nebraska and rarely responds to family attempts to contact him, although I continue to reach out to him. Of course, I flew to Nebraska to check on him and see what I could do to help him. I continue to pray for his recovery. I reach out to him often and wish him well.

AND STILL I RISE

Finding Meaning In Loss

Will the circle be unbroken, by and by Lord by and by... there's a better home awaiting, in the sky Lord in the sky – Staple Singers

Sean, Robert, Eric, and Brook, all of them had been damaged by absent or inadequate fathers, raised in an era when men weren't supposed to acknowledge pain or ask for help. They'd learned that real men tough it out, ignore symptoms, self-medicate with alcohol or drugs, or engage in dangerous behaviors.

They'd absorbed the message that vulnerability was weakness, that depending on others was shameful, that asking for medical help or emotional support was unmanly. When life became difficult, as it inevitably does, they had no tools for coping except denial, anger, and the slow suicide of self-neglect.

Jeff, Sean's father, had modeled this dysfunction perfectly. He'd abandoned his children rather than face the responsibility of supporting them, then spent decades poisoning Sean against me to avoid confronting his own failures. Sean had learned from his father that men run away from problems, blame women for their difficulties, and choose pride over survival.

The irony was that all three men, Sean, Robert, and Brook, had been intelligent, talented, capable of so much more than the lives they'd actually lived. But they'd been crippled by a culture that taught them to equate masculinity with invulnerability, to see self-care as feminine weakness rather than a necessary survival skill.

Breaking the Cycle

I'd buried both my parents, four of my brothers, and my only son. I'd watched diabetes claim Robert limb by limb, alcoholism destroy Brook's liver and brain, and medical neglect kill Sean before his time. I'd seen how untreated trauma and toxic masculinity could literally kill the people you love most.

But I'd also learned something crucial about my own power to interrupt these patterns. My grandsons would grow up with different messages about what it means to be a man. They'd learn that taking care of your health is a strength, not a weakness.

Asking for help is wisdom, not failure. Real men protect their families by protecting themselves first.

I'd broken the cycle of genetic predisposition by getting tested for BRCA1 mutations and taking preventive action. Now I needed to break the cycle of learned helplessness by teaching the next generation that survival requires both courage and care, both independence and interdependence.

Sean's daughter Alexis was already showing signs of the intelligence and determination that ran in our family line. But she was also learning, through her father's death, that smart people can make stupid decisions, that potential doesn't automatically translate into positive outcomes.

The Weight of Survival

Surviving multiple generations of family loss changes you in ways that are hard to explain to people who haven't experienced it. You develop a kind of emotional scar tissue that protects you from being completely destroyed by each new tragedy, but also makes it harder to feel joy, hope, or simple contentment.

I found myself checking on my remaining family members obsessively, calling often to make sure they were taking her medication, pestering my grandchildren about their eating habits and exercise routines.

The hyper vigilance that had kept me alive through decades of crisis had become a permanent state of mind.

Watching people you love die from preventable causes creates a kind of urgency, a desperate need to do something, anything to prevent the next tragedy.

Even when logic tells you that adults make their own choices, even when experience proves that you can't love someone into making better decisions.

Gradually, over the months following Sean's death, I began to understand that the meaning of my losses wasn't in preventing them, it was in learning from them, honoring them, using them to build something better for future generations.

Sean's passing taught me about the deadly consequences of untreated trauma and toxic masculinity. Robert's decline showed me how denial and enabling can kill people who might have been saved by intervention and accountability. Brook's final years demonstrated the importance of early treatment for addiction and mental health issues.

Happy Ending

While there is no such thing as "happily ever after" or "happy ending", this book provides a strong and loving voice, still standing despite so much heartbreak and loss. The lessons contained herein are offered as encouragement and support to those of us who have family and loved ones who suffer from the disease of addiction. Please be aware that one can overcome any obstacle, be it in the form of addiction, health, or lifestyle choices, but you must push very hard against obstacles, seen and unseen.

It is entirely possible to live life fully and gain the benefit of a higher consciousness that comes from living life on purpose. Stand on faith that there is a loving God, fully capable, merciful, and compassionate. You will succeed, guaranteed!

FOR YOU

A Note From Janet

Everything in this book happened. I did not write it to impress you, and I did not write it to frighten you. I wrote it because I needed you to understand how quickly a life can unravel when the right information arrives too late — or never arrives at all.

My mother died of ovarian cancer. She never knew about genetic testing. My brother Robert lost his limbs to diabetes, one by one, over the years of infections that better home care could have caught early. My son Sean had three strokes before he died at fifty-two — strokes that his doctors told him were coming, that I begged him to prevent, that a different relationship with his own health might have stopped.

I watched every one of them go. I watched them go, knowing there were resources, programs, phone numbers, and people whose entire job it is to help — and that none of my loved ones ever reached them.

So I put together what follows. Not as an afterthought. As the other half of this book.

The Resource Guide is organized by the challenges that appear most often in the stories on these pages — health, housing, legal matters, financial assistance, and support for seniors. If something in this memoir made you think of someone you love, start there. If something made you think of yourself, start there, too.

You have already done the hardest part. You picked up the book. You read the whole thing. Now use it.

— Janet Pinkney

Resource Guide & Glossary

God Bless the Child That's Got His Own

Purpose: This glossary provides easy access to vital information for addressing many of today's challenges. It serves as a starting point, enabling readers to consider various options and the actions required to access needed goods and services.

Health Resources for Women

Adoption Services

Adoption.com - Unplanned Pregnancy Resources
Website: https://adoption.com/unplanned-pregnancy/

Florence Crittenton Services
Home for unwed mothers
Website: https://florencecrittentonhome.com/stateinfo.html

Annie E. Casey Foundation
Phone: 410-547-6600
Address: 701 St. Paul St., Baltimore, MD 21202
Website: https://www.aecf.org/topics/foster-care

Family Planning & Healthcare

United Way
Call 211 to connect to services
Website: 211.org

Planned Parenthood
Website: https://www.plannedparenthood.org/
Abortion Finder: https://www.abortionfinder.org/

Health Care Marketplace
Website: Healthcare.gov
Phone: 1-800-318-2596

Breast Health

Susan G. Komen Foundation
Breast Care Helpline: 1-877-465-6636 (1-877-GO-KOMEN)
Email: helpline@komen.org
Website: https://www.komen.org/support-resources/breast-can-cer-helpline/

Health Resources for Children

Centers for Medicare & Medicaid Services
Website: https://www.medicaid.gov/about-us/Center-for-Medic-aid-and-CHIP-Services/index.html
Toll-Free: 877-267-2323

Kidney Disease Resources

National Kidney Foundation
Main Number: (800) 622-9010
Email: info@kidney.org

NKF Cares
Phone: 855-653-2273 (855-NKF-CARES)
Email: nkfcares@kidney.org
Website: https://www.kidney.org/about/kidney-disease-fact-sheet

Important Facts:

- About 9 in 10 adults with kidney disease (~90%) do not know they have it

- Chronic kidney disease (CKD) causes more deaths each year than breast cancer or prostate cancer
- It is an under-recognized public health crisis

Section 8 & Housing Assistance

Families in Foreclosure
Phone: 855-917-2405

US Department of Housing and Urban Development (HUD)
Housing Choice Voucher Program (Section 8):

- https://www.hud.gov/topics/housing_choice_voucher_program_section_8
- https://www.hud.gov/program_offices/public_indian_housing/programs/hcv/about

Senior Housing Information
Website: https://www.hud.gov/topics/information_for_senior_citizens

Additional Resources:

- https://en.uslowcosthousing.com/posts/how-can-i-apply-for-section-8-online-and-qualify-for-it/
- https://en.uslowcosthousing.com/posts/a-step-by-step-guide-for-section-8-housing/

Catholic Charities Housing Services

Services Provided:

- Disaster relief
- Immigration help
- Emergency rent payments
- Housing counseling (pre-purchase, foreclosure prevention)
- Fair housing workshops
- Predatory lending education
- Financial education

Contact Information:
Address: 2050 Ballenger Ave, Suite 400, Alexandria, VA 22314
Phone: 703-549-1390
Email: info@catholiccharitiesusa.org

Legal Resources

General Legal Help

Legal FAQ
Website: https://legalfaq.org/
Provides resources for eviction, foreclosure, and other legal matters

Just Answer Court
Free legal advice resource
Website: https://www.justanswer.com/

American Bar Association
Each state has its own Bar Association - the governing body for attorneys. Contact your state's bar association to find attorneys and compare legal fees.

The Innocence Project

Mission: National litigation and public policy organization dedicated to exonerating wrongfully convicted individuals through

DNA testing and other scientific advancements, and reforming the criminal justice system.

Founded: 1992 by Barry C. Scheck and Peter J. Neufeld at the Benjamin N. Cardozo School of Law at Yeshiva University

Contact Information:
Phone: 212-364-5340
Email: info@innocenceproject.org
Press: press@innocenceproject.org
Submit a Case: https://innocenceproject.org/submit-case/

Paralegal Services

Paralegals can draft and file documents in State and Magistrate courts at reasonable fees, often much cheaper than hiring an attorney. While paralegals cannot represent you in court, they can help you file "Pro Se" (representing yourself). Most experienced paralegals are well-versed in legal jurisprudence. Conduct a Google search to locate paralegals in your area.

Financial Assistance

Finance Buzz - Rent Assistance Resources
Website: https://financebuzz.com/legit-ways-to-help-pay-rent-yaez

Patient Assistance - Prescription Help Programs
Phone: (866) 326-6063

Consumer Protection

Consumer Protection Agency
Phone: 301-604-3305
Website: https://www.usa.gov/state-consumer

Consumer Affairs Department

Find local help in your city, state, or county:

- https://countyinfo.hoursguide.com/offices/
- https://countyinfo.hoursguide.com/consumer-affairs-department

Domestic Violence Resources

National Domestic Violence Hotline

Phone: 1-800-799-7233

Text: "START" to 88788

About the Hotline:

Every contact is confidential and personal. The hotline serves survivors of abuse, concerned friends or family members, and abusive partners seeking to change themselves.

Important Statistics:

Most female victims of intimate partner violence were previously victimized by the same offender at rates of 77% for women ages 18-24, 76% for ages 25-34, and 81% for ages 35-49.

Source: http://www.ncjrs.gov/App/publications/abstract.aspx?ID=261262

Resources for Seniors

Administration for Community Living

Website: acl.gov

The "Older Adults" section provides links to:

- State and local services for older adults and families
- Public and private benefits programs

- Medicare
- Long-term care planning

211/United Way
Dial: 211
Website: 211.org
Connect to a call center that can help refer you to affordable housing and other community resources.

Administration on Aging
Website: aoa.gov
Phone: 1-800-677-1116
Helps people find care for senior loved ones.

Eldercare.gov
Website: eldercare.gov
Provides fact sheets, booklets, and links for federal websites.

National Council on Aging
Website: ncoa.org
Additional site: benefitscheckup.org
Provides a list of federal and state assistance programs.

New Lifestyles
Website: newlifestyles.com
Information on senior residences and care options.

Volunteers of America
Website: voa.org
Helps search for affordable housing and provides vital support services.

Visiting Nurse Associations of America
Website: vnaa.org
Non-profit agency devoted to helping people find home and hospice care for loved ones.

Autism Speaks
Phone: 888-288-4762 (888-AUTISM2)
Email: help@autismspeaks.org
Website: autismspeaks.org

Georgia Regional BSV
Caregiver Portal: https://garegionalbsvc.com/caregiver-portal

Education & Financial Aid

US Department of Education
Website: https://www.ed.gov/
Federal Student Aid: https://studentaid.gov/

Scholarship Resources

Alpha Kappa Alpha Sorority, Incorporated
AKA EOO Scholarship Application (High School 2025)

FastWeb – Scholarship Network
Virtual clearinghouse for most available scholarships nationwide
Website: https://www.fastweb.com/

Sallie Mae Scholarships
No-essay scholarships: https://www.sallie.com/scholarships/no-essay
General scholarships: https://www.sallie.com/scholarships/scholly

This resource guide is provided as a reference tool. Please verify contact information and eligibility requirements before accessing services.

About the Author

WALKING ON BROKEN GLASS

Prodigal Child Returns

Janet Pinkney continues to be a strong advocate for the under-privileged in her own family and in the community at large. She heads a non-profit organization named in honor of her book "Walking on Broken Glass." The organization serves as a hub and a much-needed resource for underserved people, helplessly caught in the deadly undertow of life's harsh circumstances.

While many life events are often the result of unforeseen circumstances, they are mostly the result of several competing factors, bad decisions, genetics or just plain dumb luck; these matters need to be addressed and acknowledged constructively. Once managed divisively and aggressively, these matters will help ensure a healthy, viable outcome for everyone. She firmly believes that everyone deserves at least a chance at a wholesome, healthy life.

Currently, Janet is a sought-after speaker at hospitals, schools, churches, programs for teenage mothers, as well as many other groups who are joined in the fight to access to affordable health care. She has been a well-respected health and life insurance producer since receiving her insurance license in 2008, working closely with major health insurance companies to ensure that patients obtain the best care available. She uses her expertise to help individuals navigate the rigors of the Health Care system in the United States. Typically, these matters can determine if a person lives or dies, largely depending upon the level of care one receives.

While this is a well-known fact, few in the Health Care industry actually address this matter, while thousands die daily from lack of access to urgently needed health care.

Janet is also the host of a weekly podcast, "Ask Janet", which provides an open forum where anyone can obtain clear, consistent advice and direction while facing tough circumstances.

She enjoys spending time with her beloved grandchildren and enjoys her role as a great-grandmother, to her growing brood of youngsters...a true blessing.